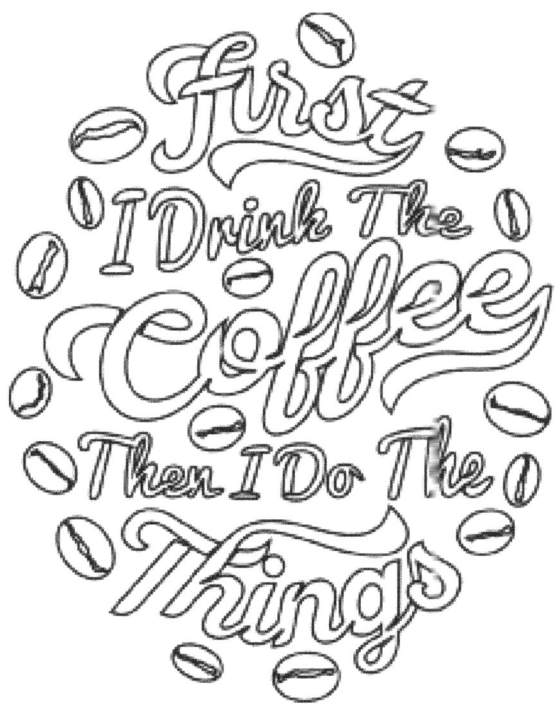

THIS COLORING BOOK BELONGS TO

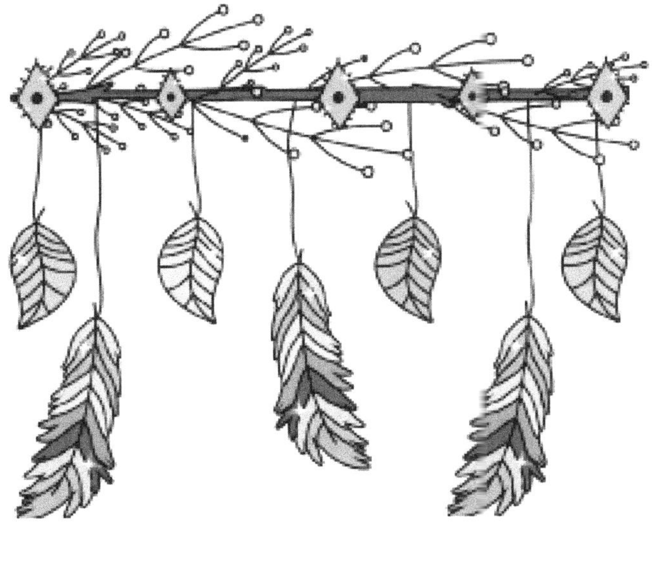

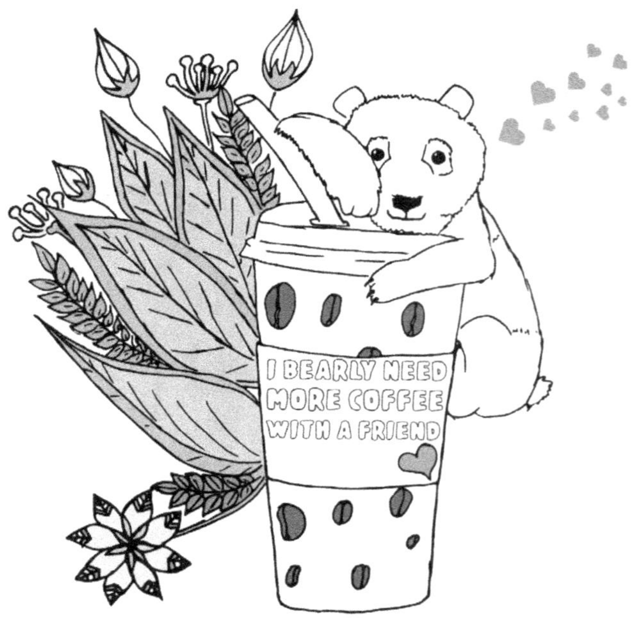
I BEARLY NEED
MORE COFFEE
WITH A FRIEND

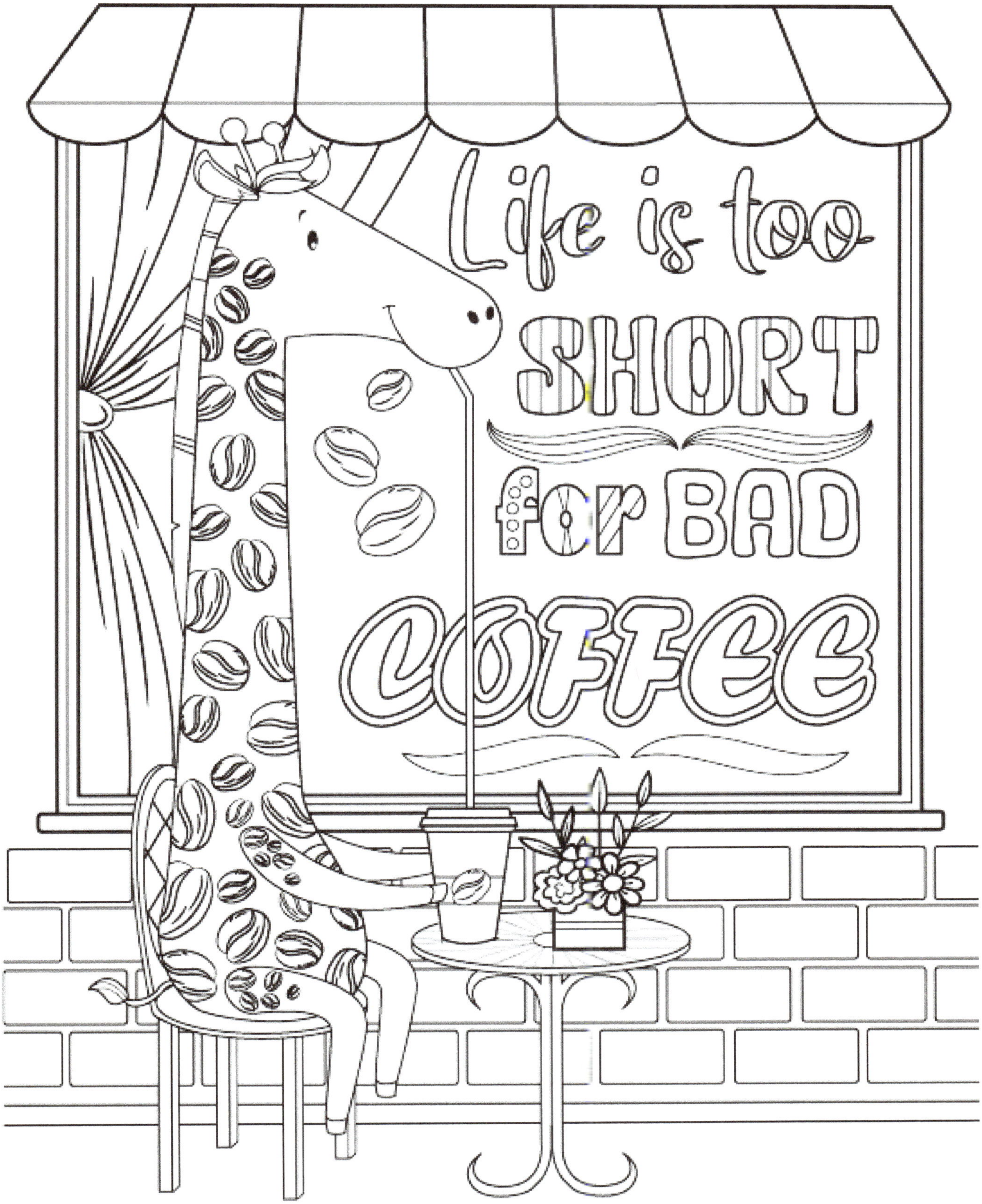
Life is too
SHORT
for BAD
COFFEE

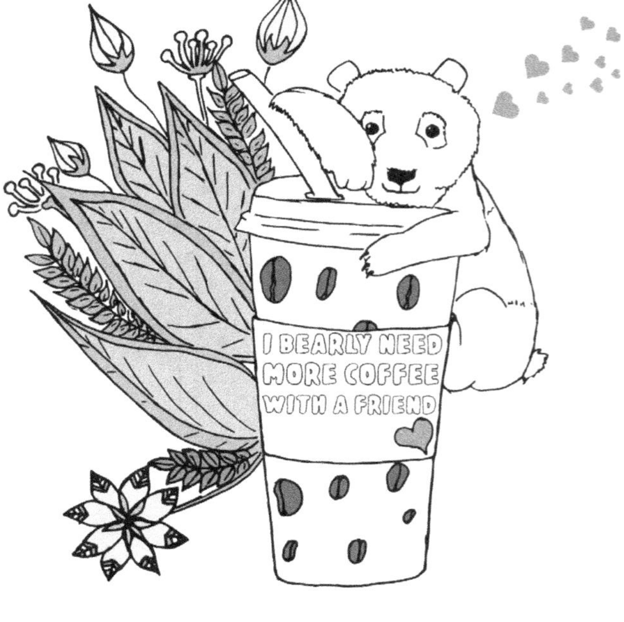
I BEARLY NEED
MORE COFFEE
WITH A FRIEND

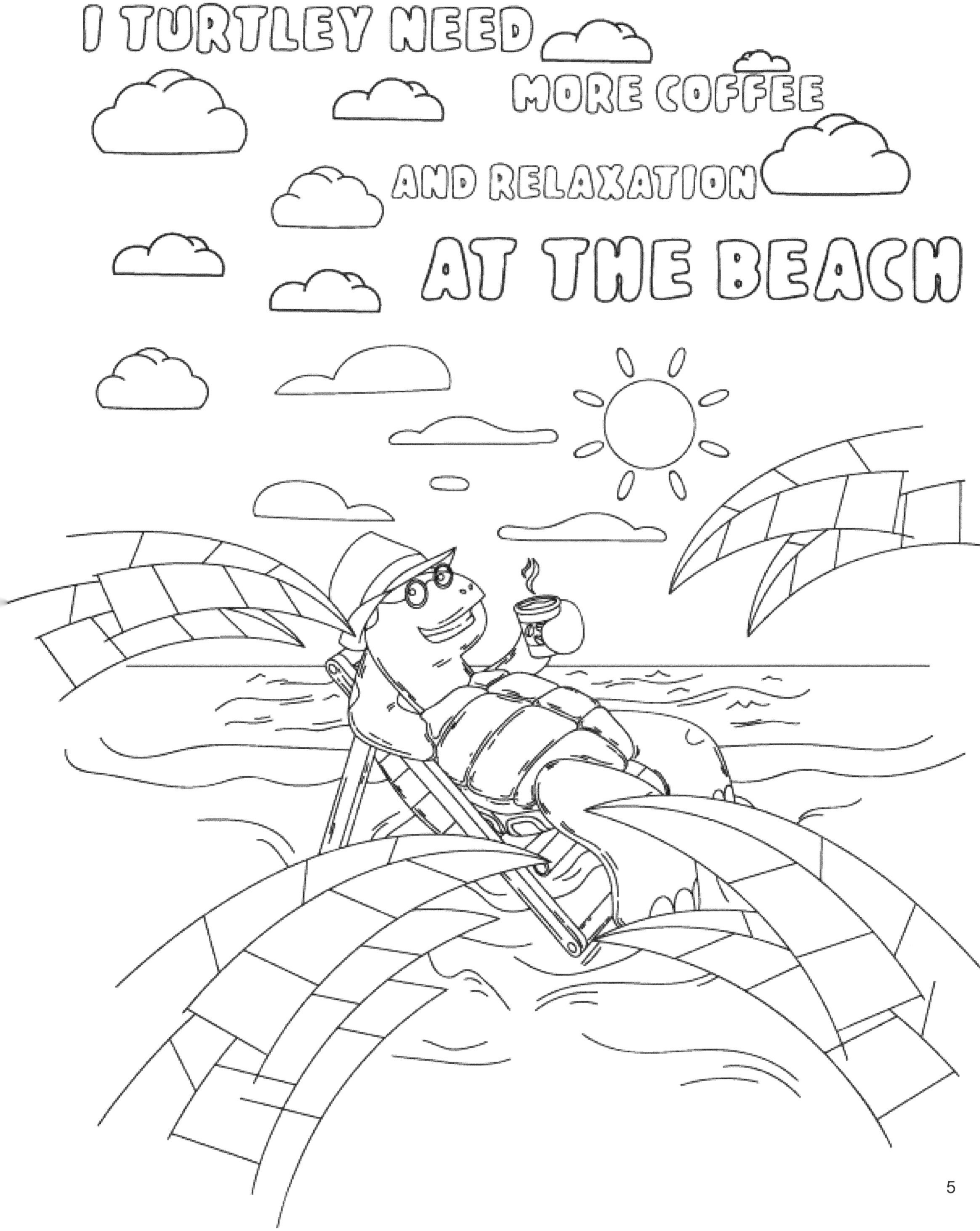
I TURTLEY NEED
MORE COFFEE
AND RELAXATION
AT THE BEACH

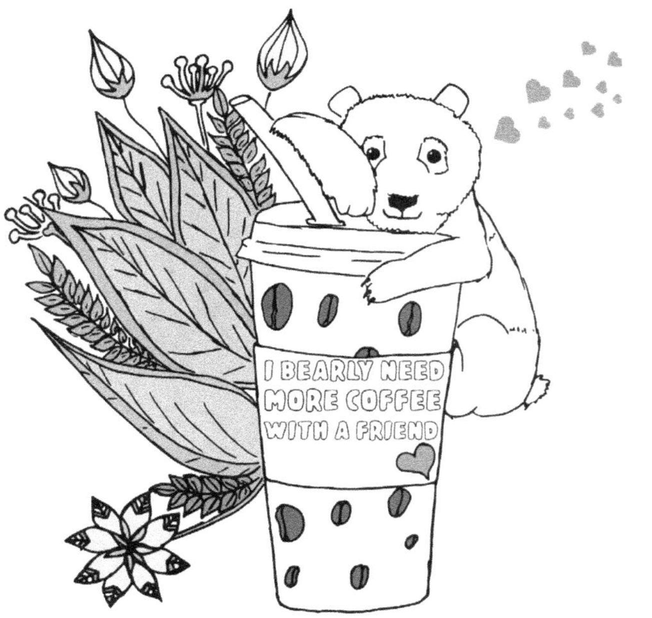
I BEARLY NEED
MORE COFFEE
WITH A FRIEND

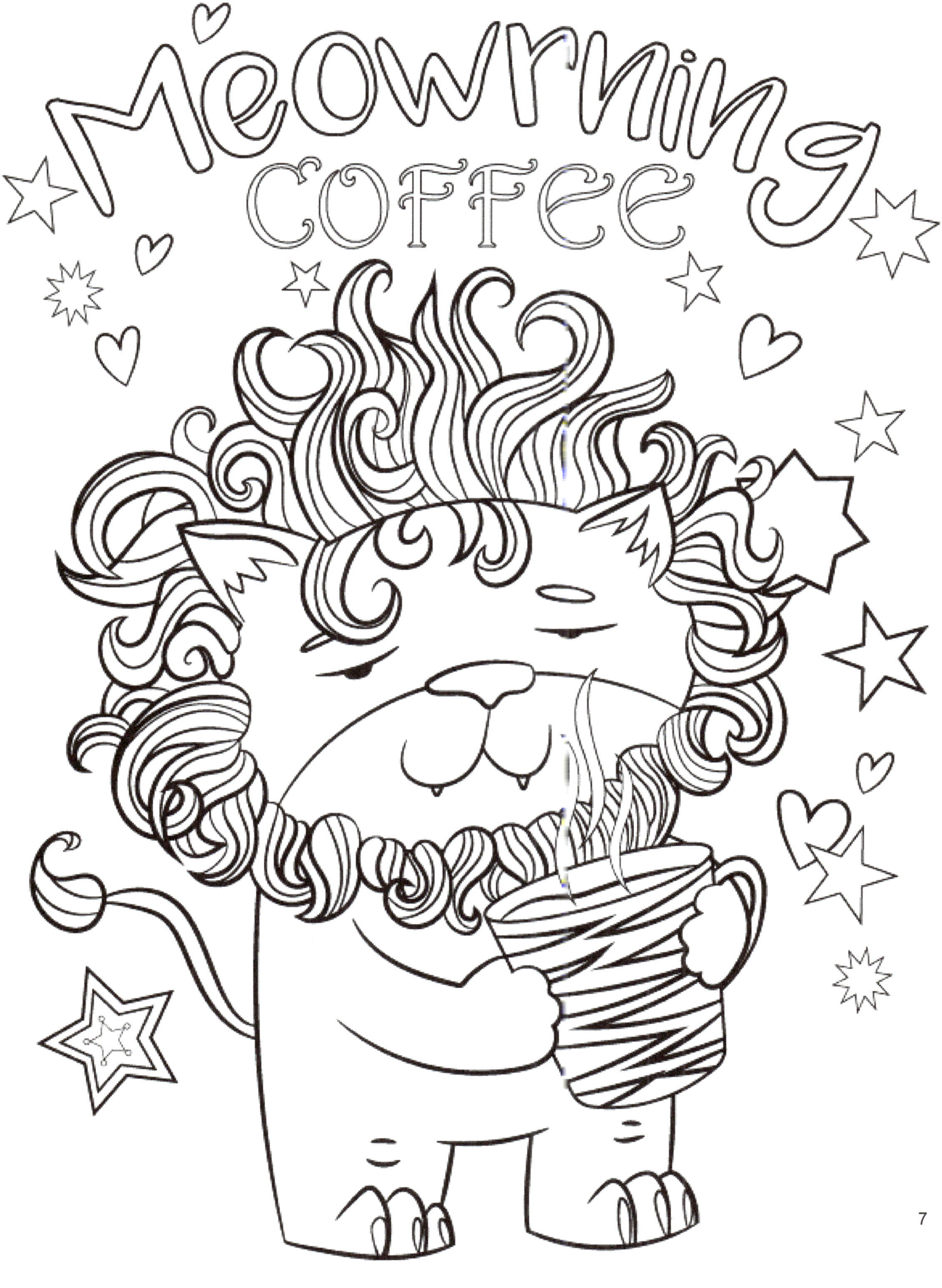
Meowrning
coffee

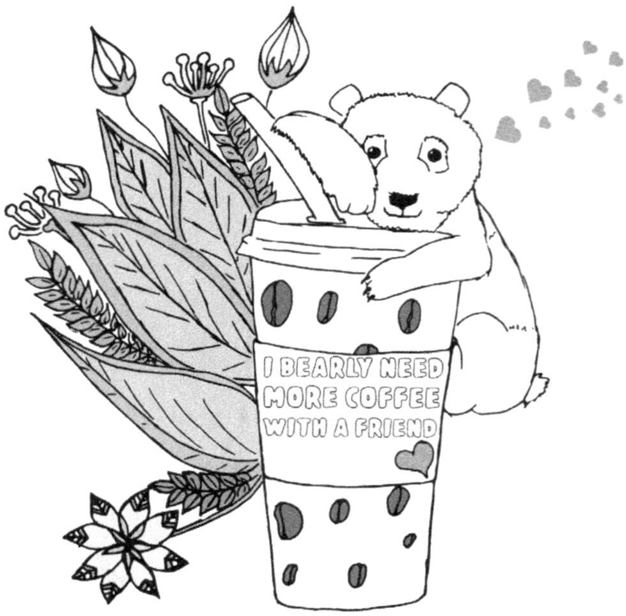
I BEARLY NEED
MORE COFFEE
WITH A FRIEND

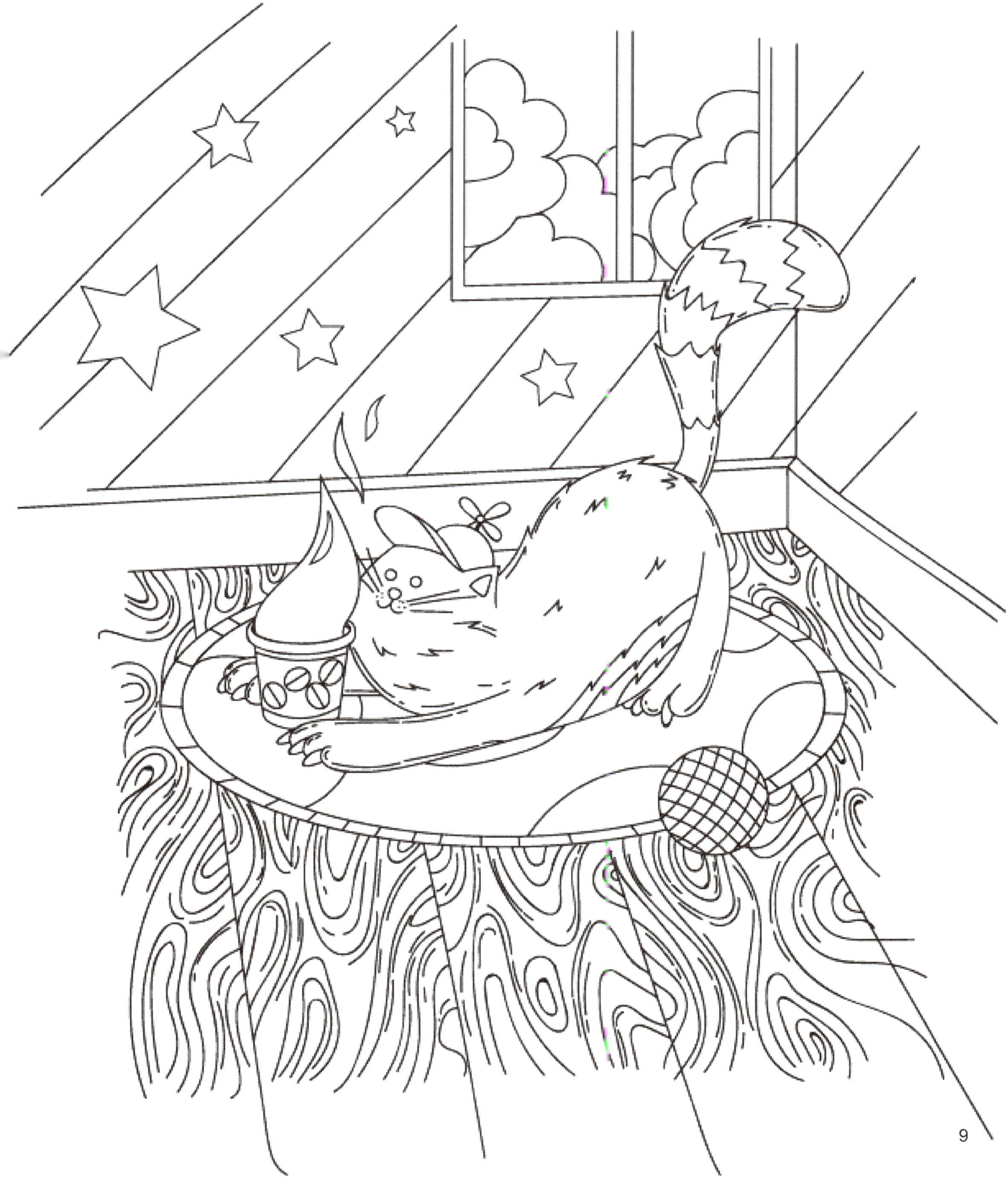

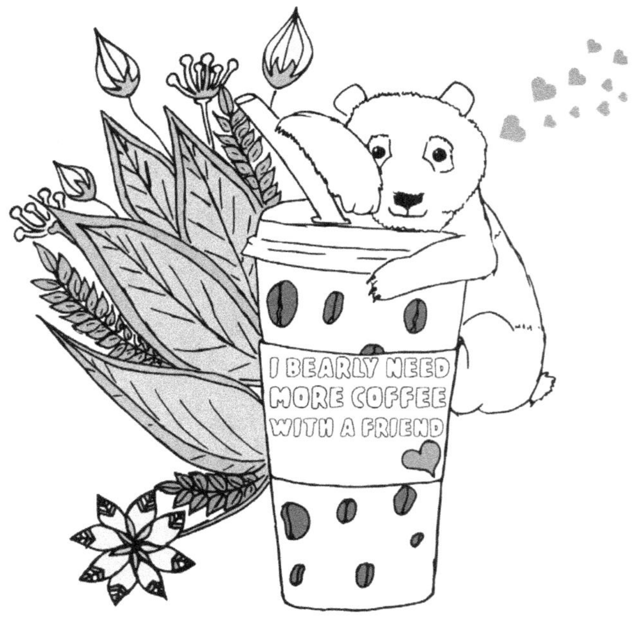
I BEARLY NEED
MORE COFFEE
WITH A FRIEND

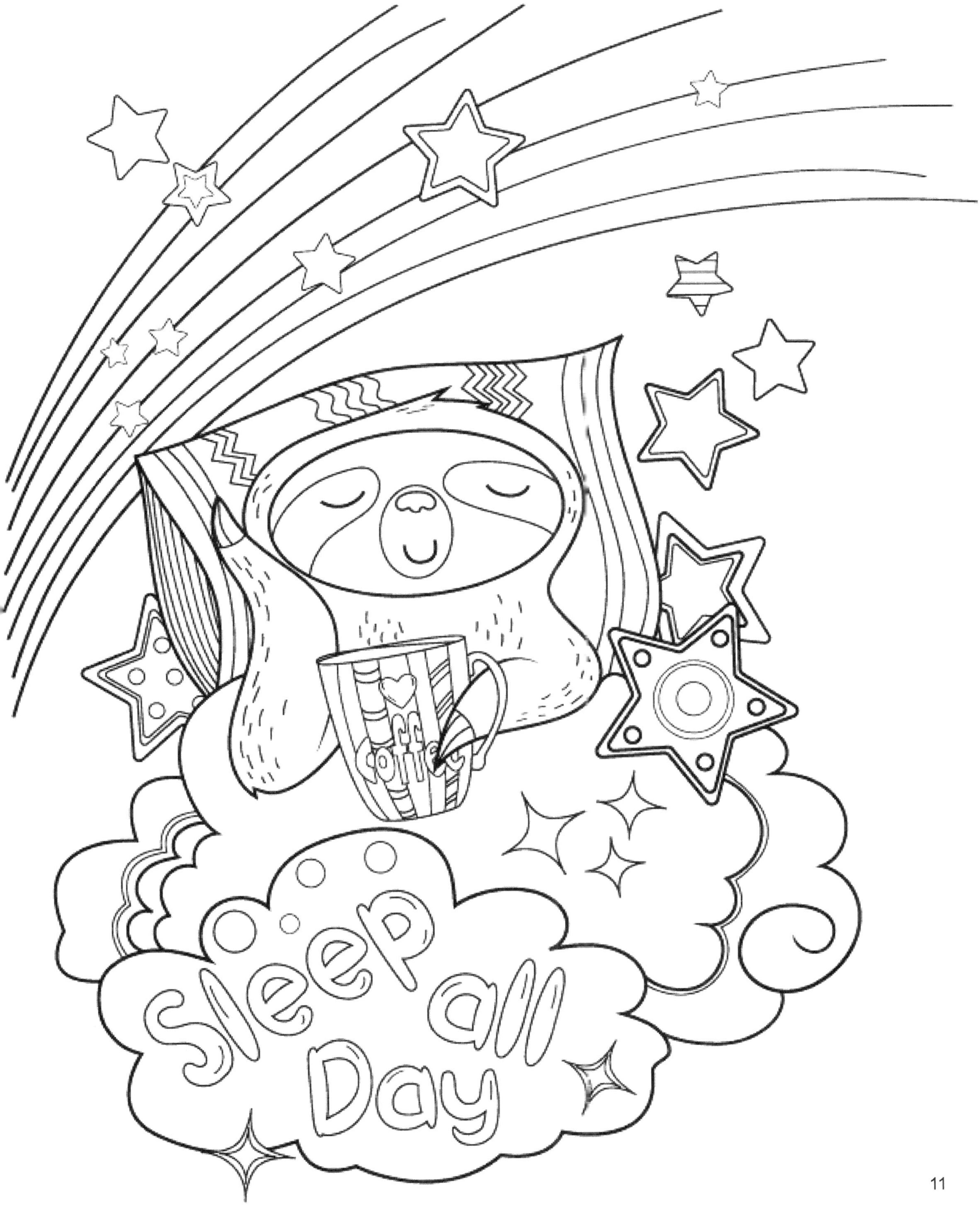
coffee
Sleep all
Day

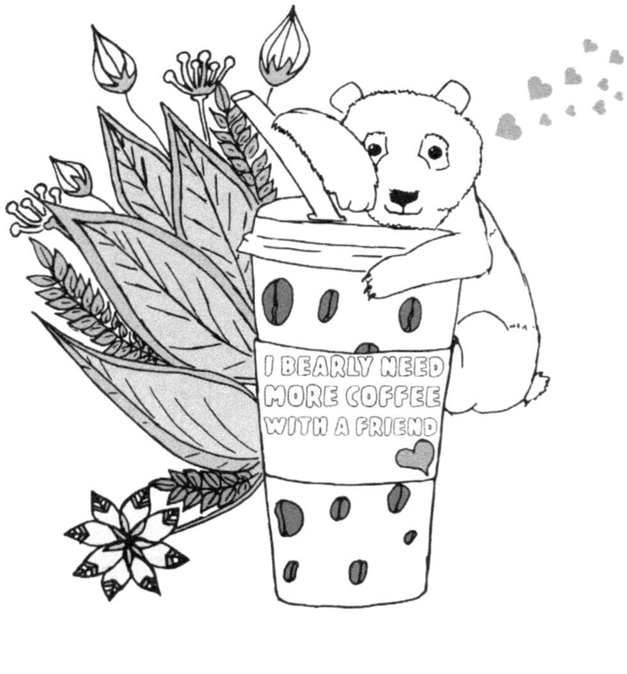
I BEARLY NEED
MORE COFFEE
WITH A FRIEND

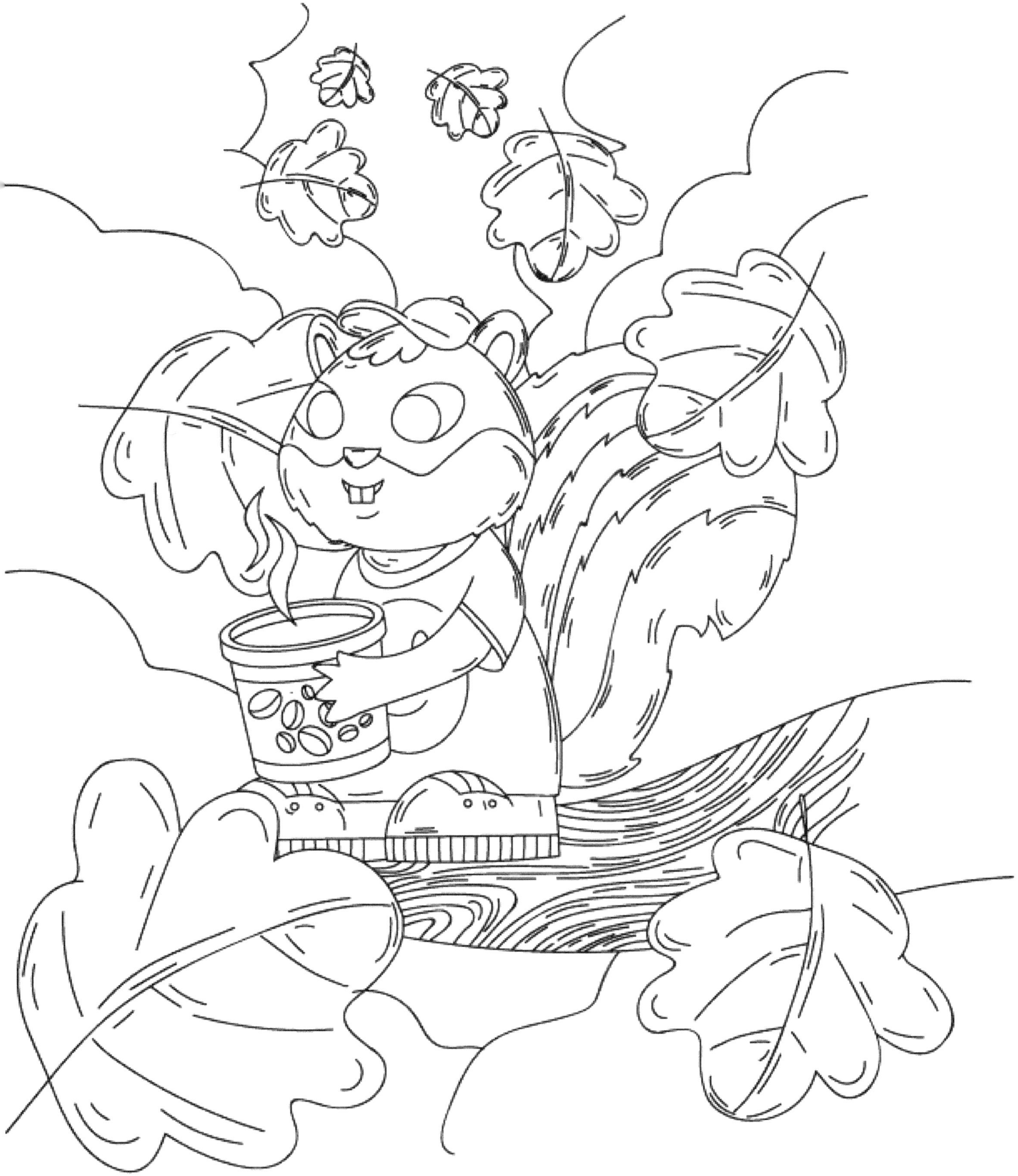

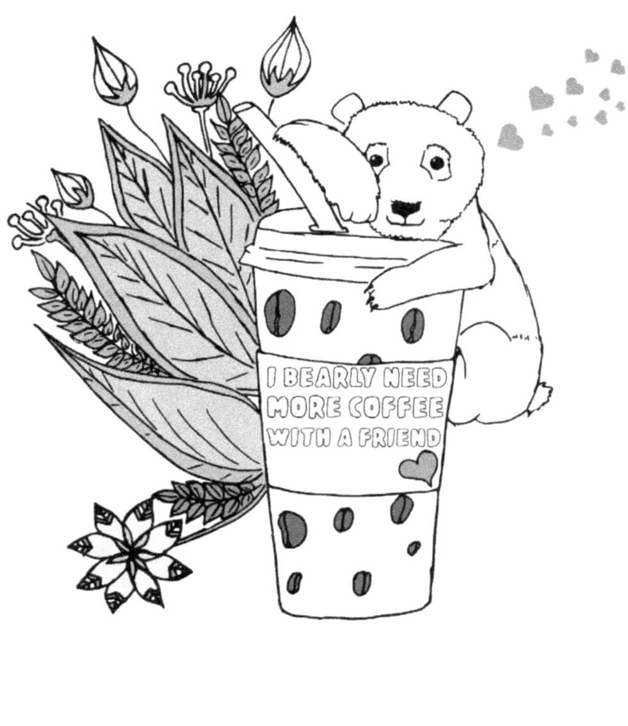
I BEARLY NEED
MORE COFFEE
WITH A FRIEND

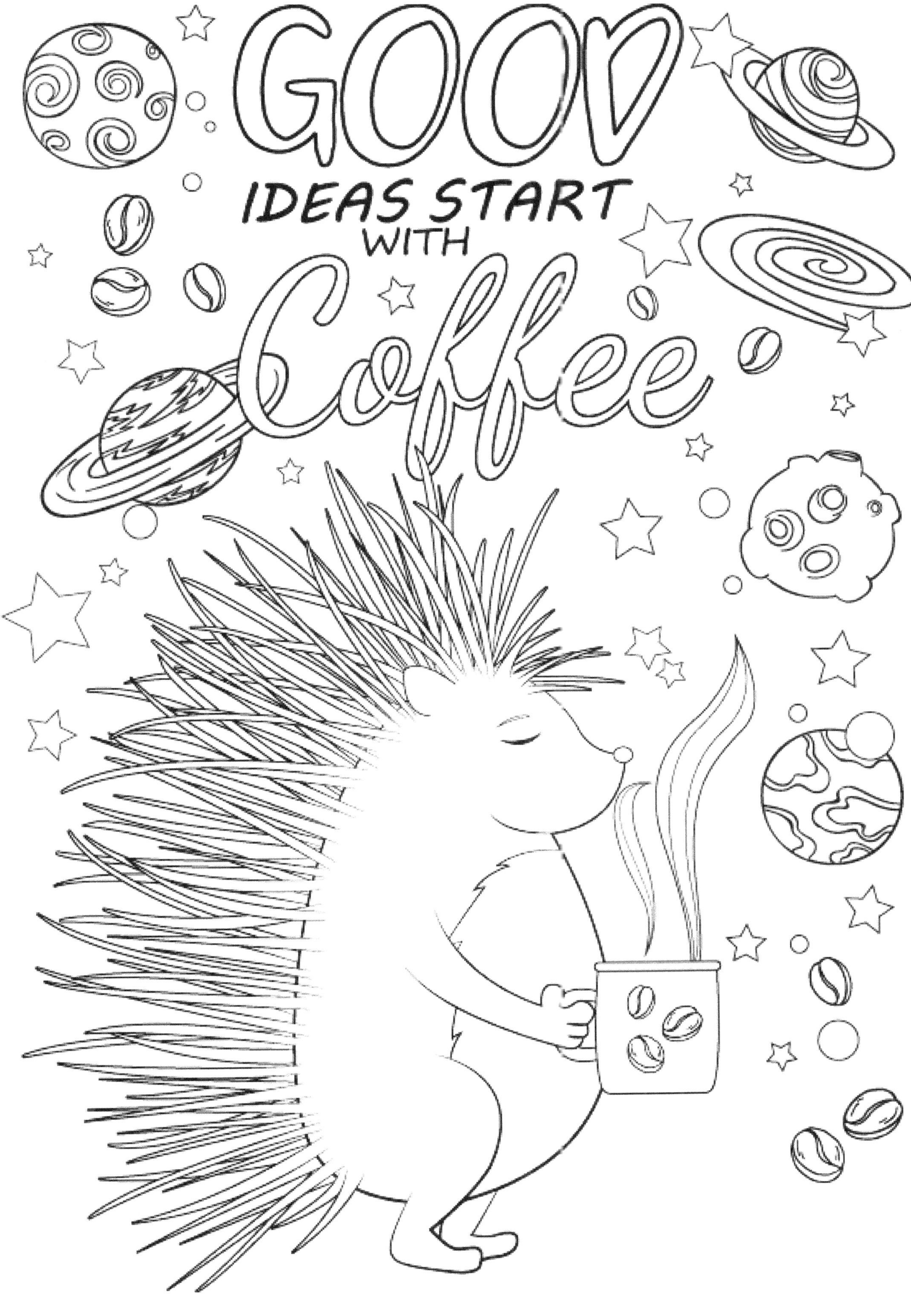
GOOD
IDEAS START
WITH
Coffee

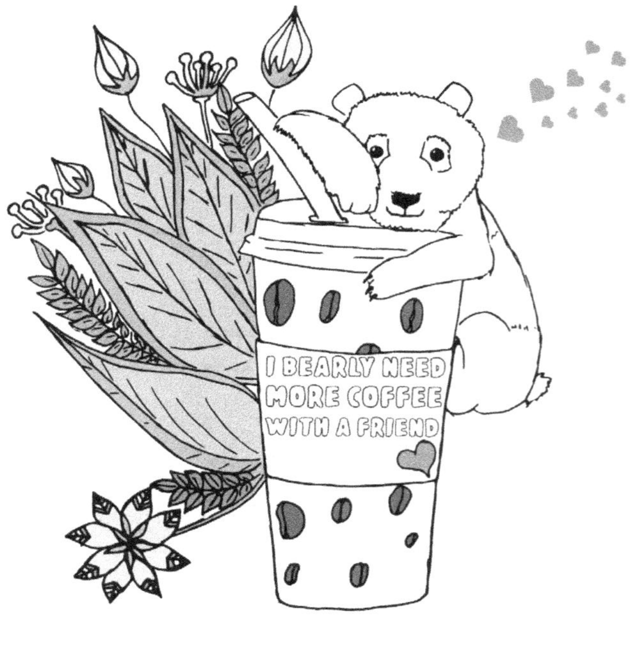
I BEARLY NEED
MORE COFFEE
WITH A FRIEND

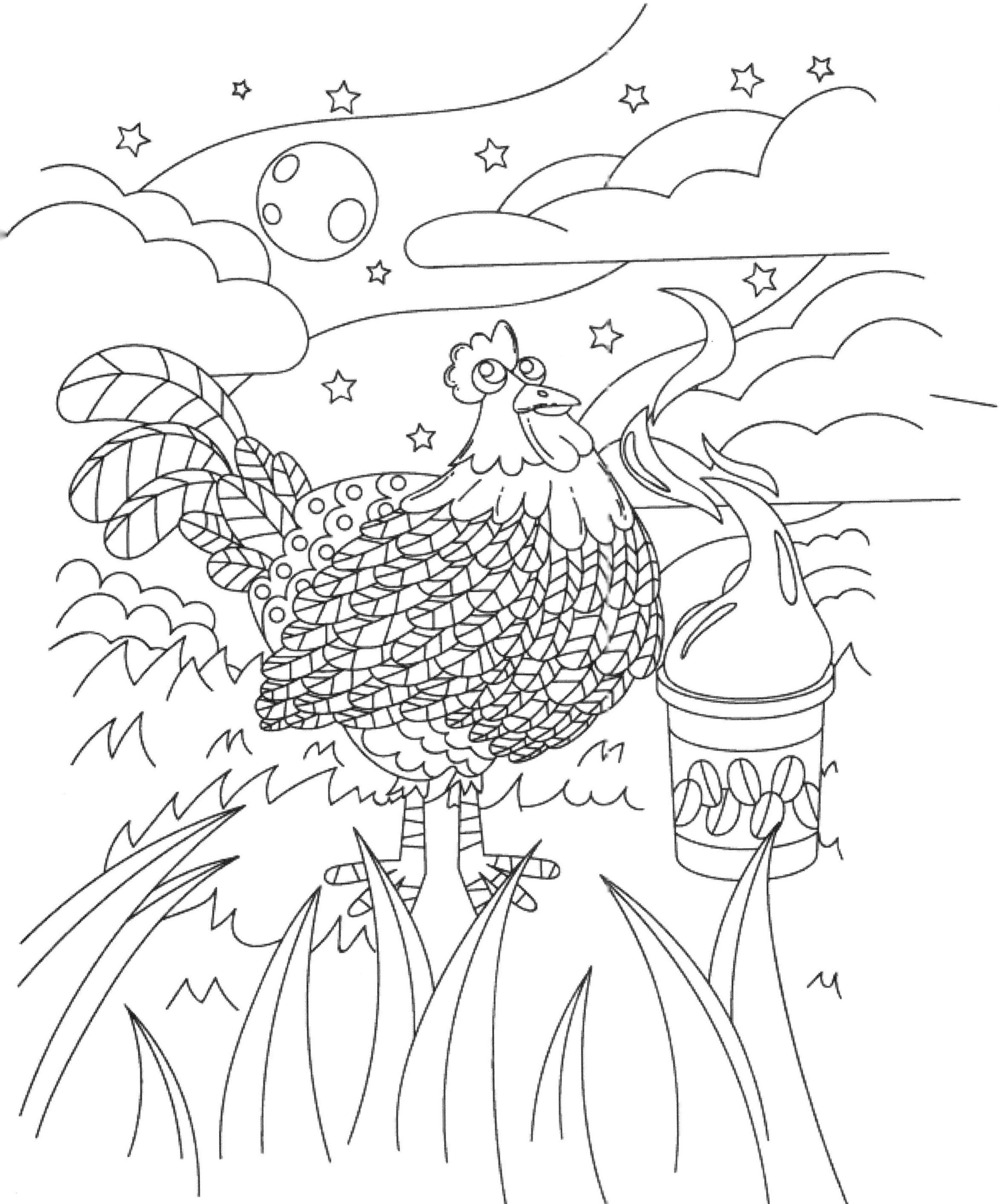

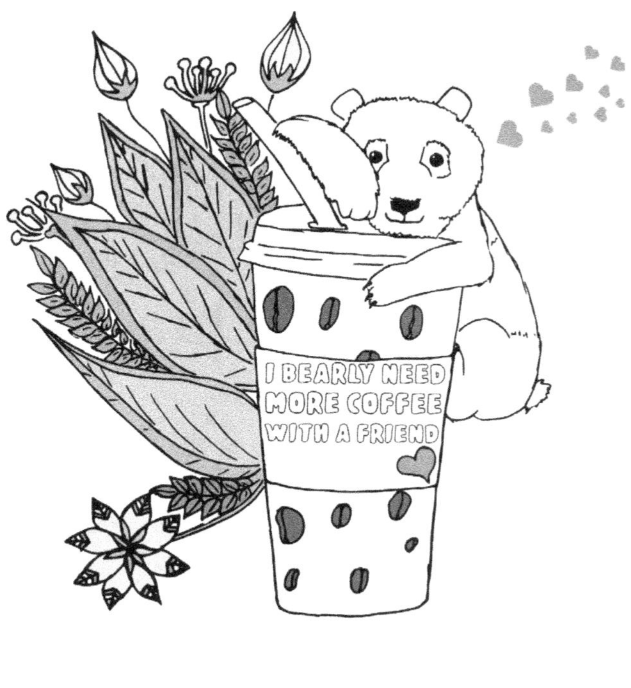
I BEARLY NEED
MORE COFFEE
WITH A FRIEND

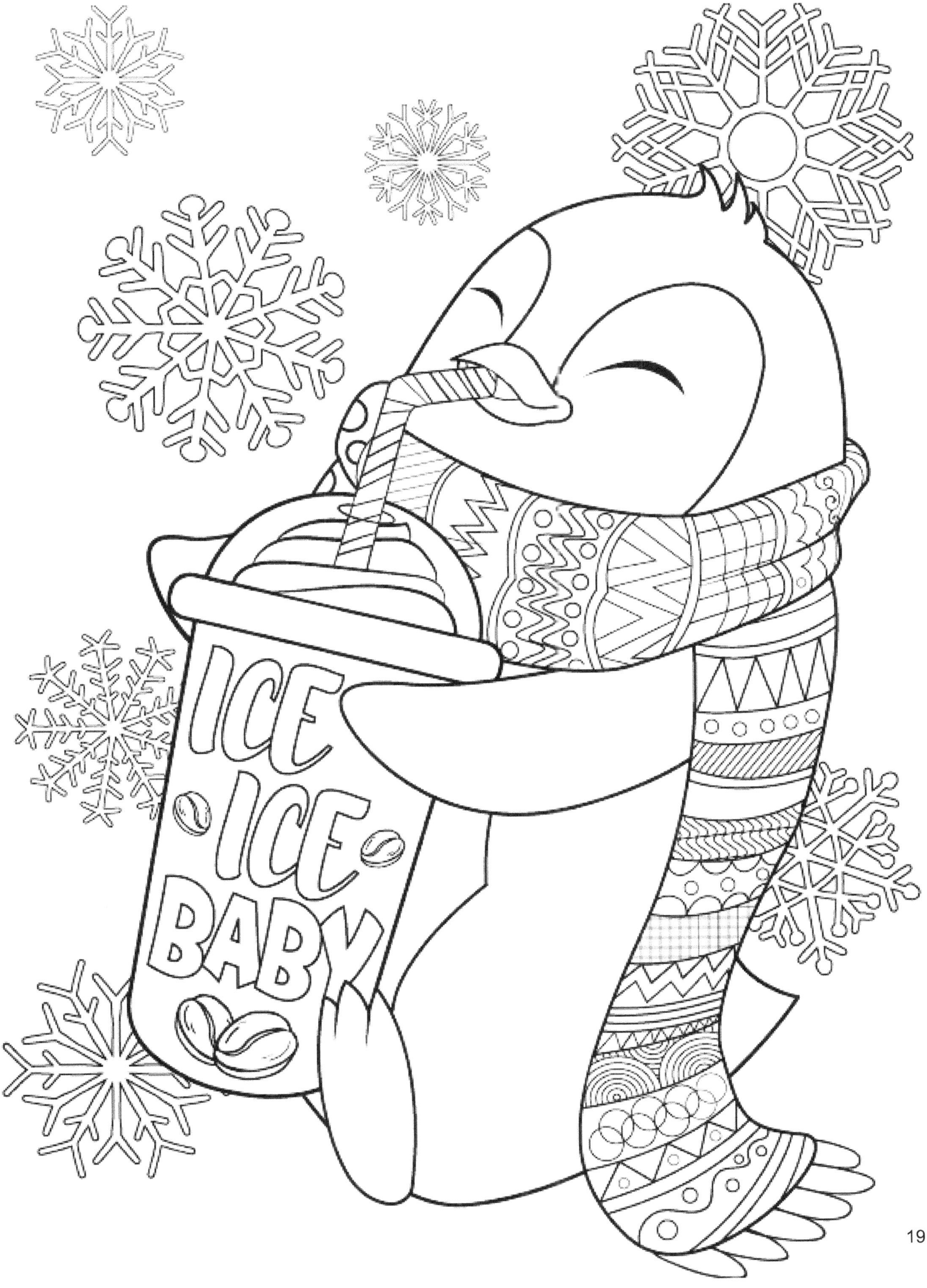
ICE
ICE
ICE
BABY

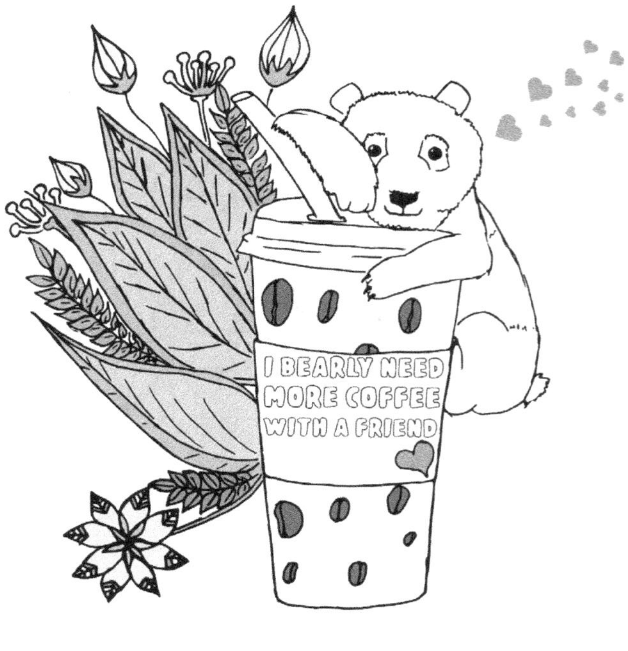
I BEARLY NEED
MORE COFFEE
WITH A FRIEND

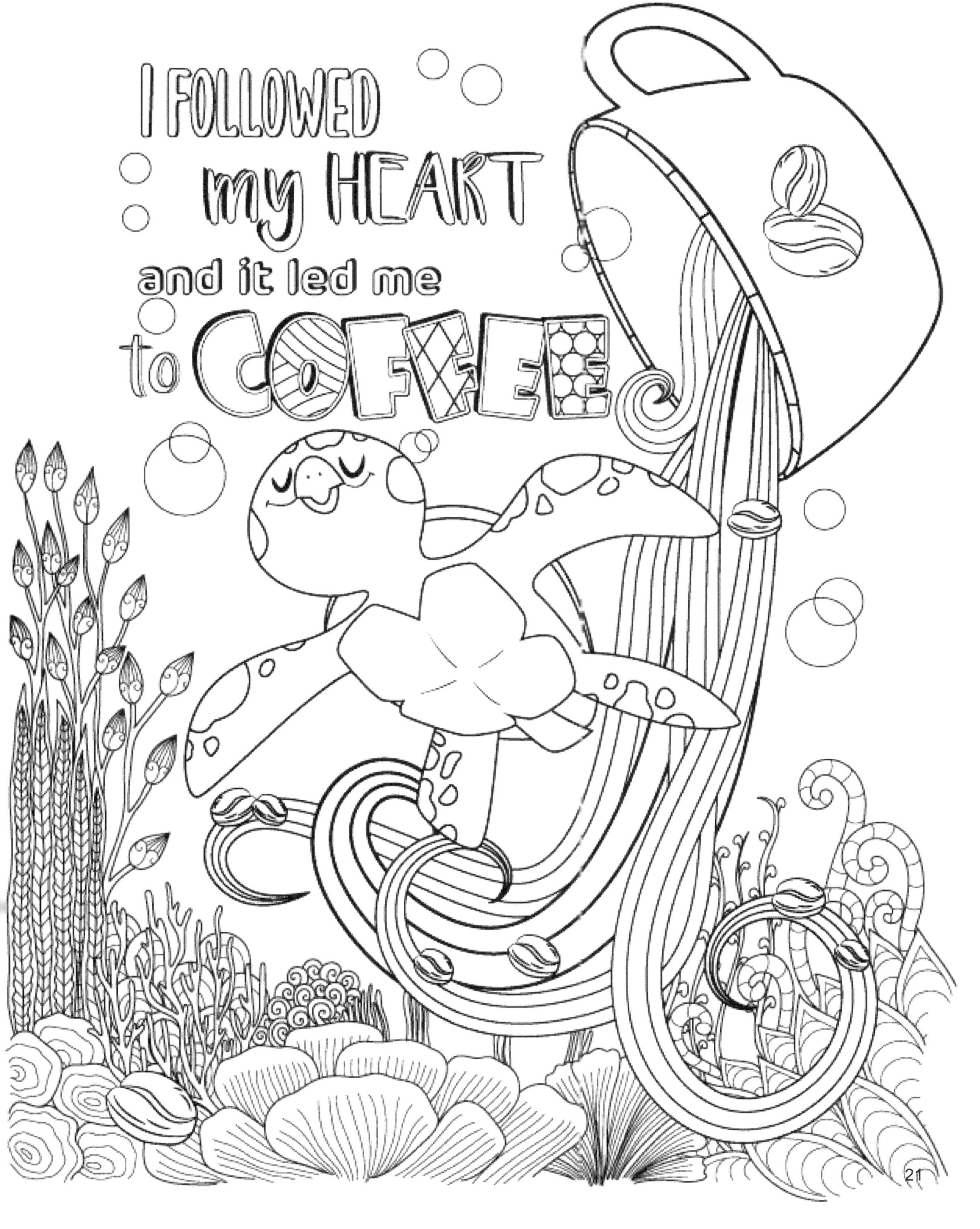
I FOLLOWED
my HEART
and it led me
to COFFEE

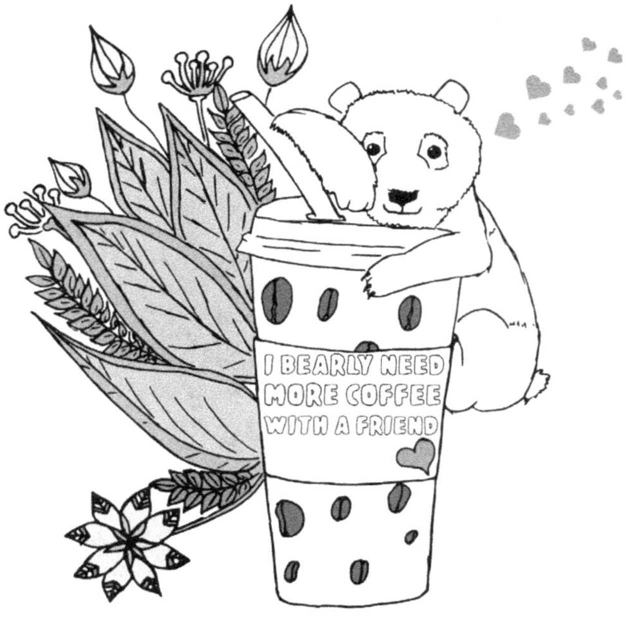
I BEARLY NEED
MORE COFFEE
WITH A FRIEND

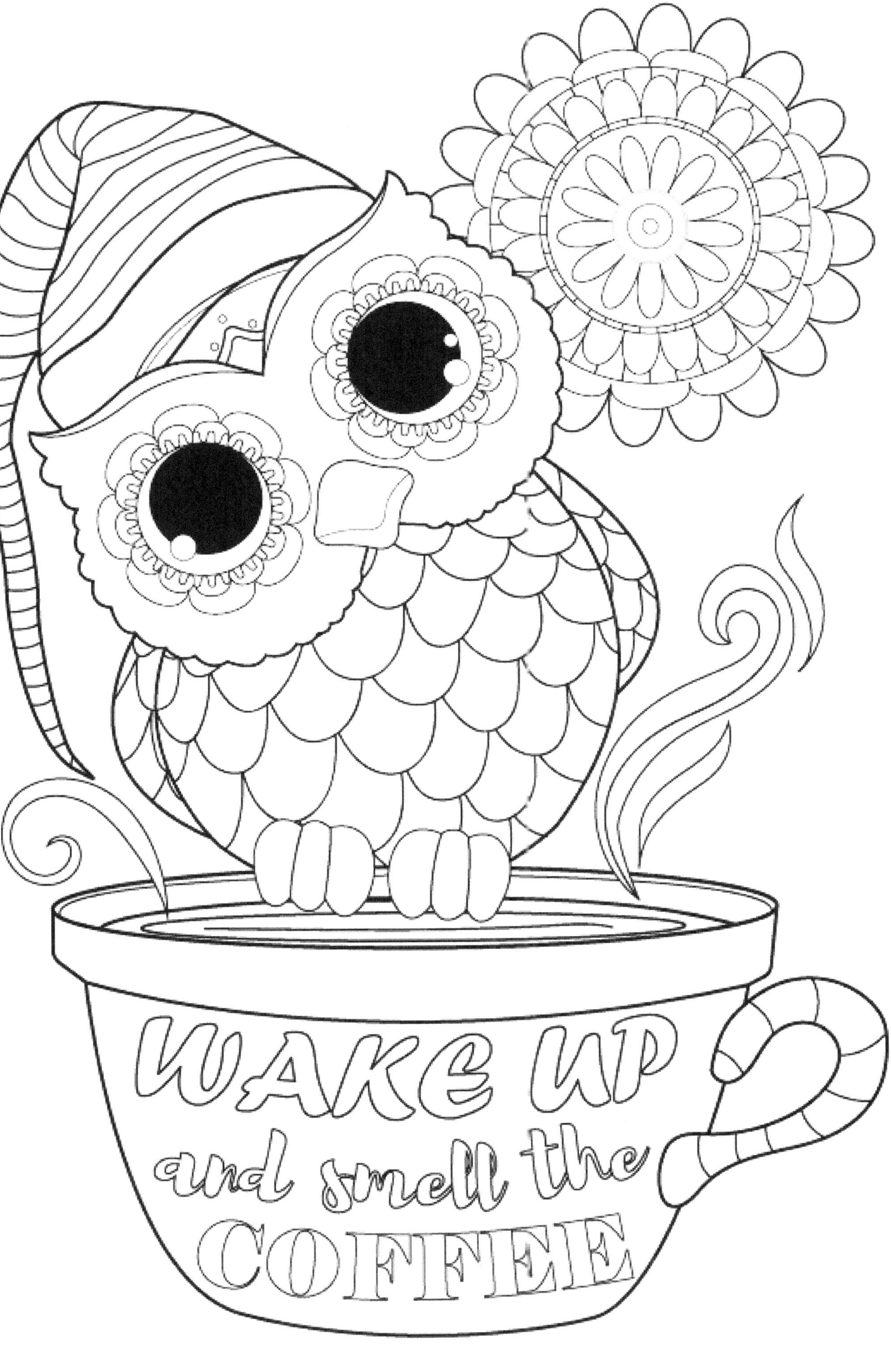
WAKE UP
and smell the
COFFEE

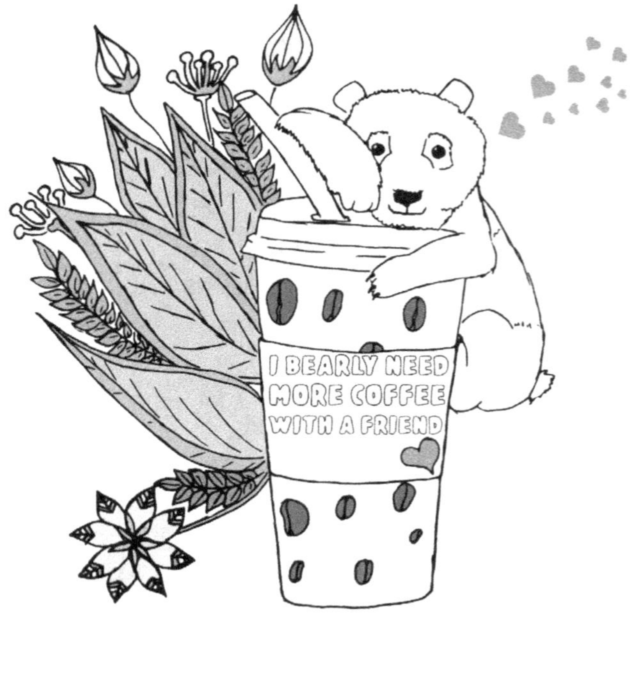
I BEARLY NEED
MORE COFFEE
WITH A FRIEND

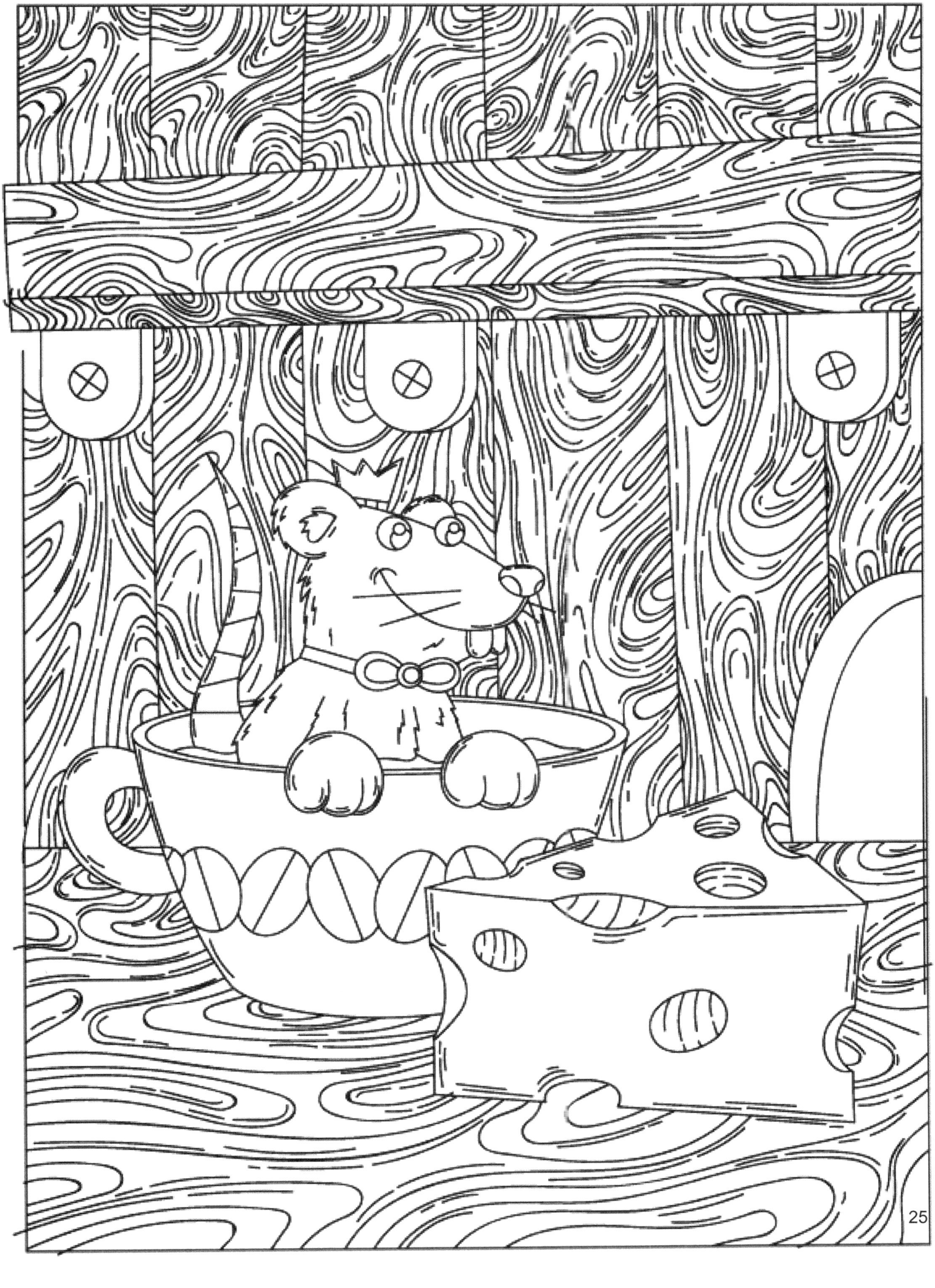

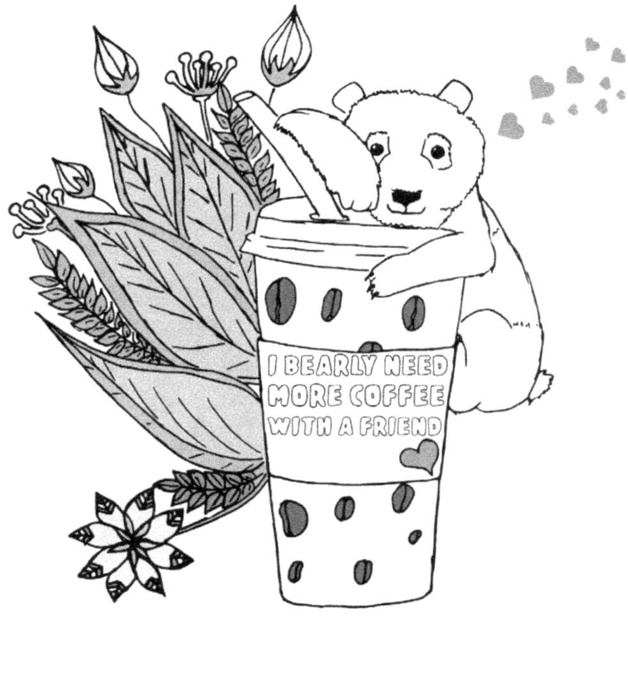
I BEARLY NEED
MORE COFFEE
WITH A FRIEND

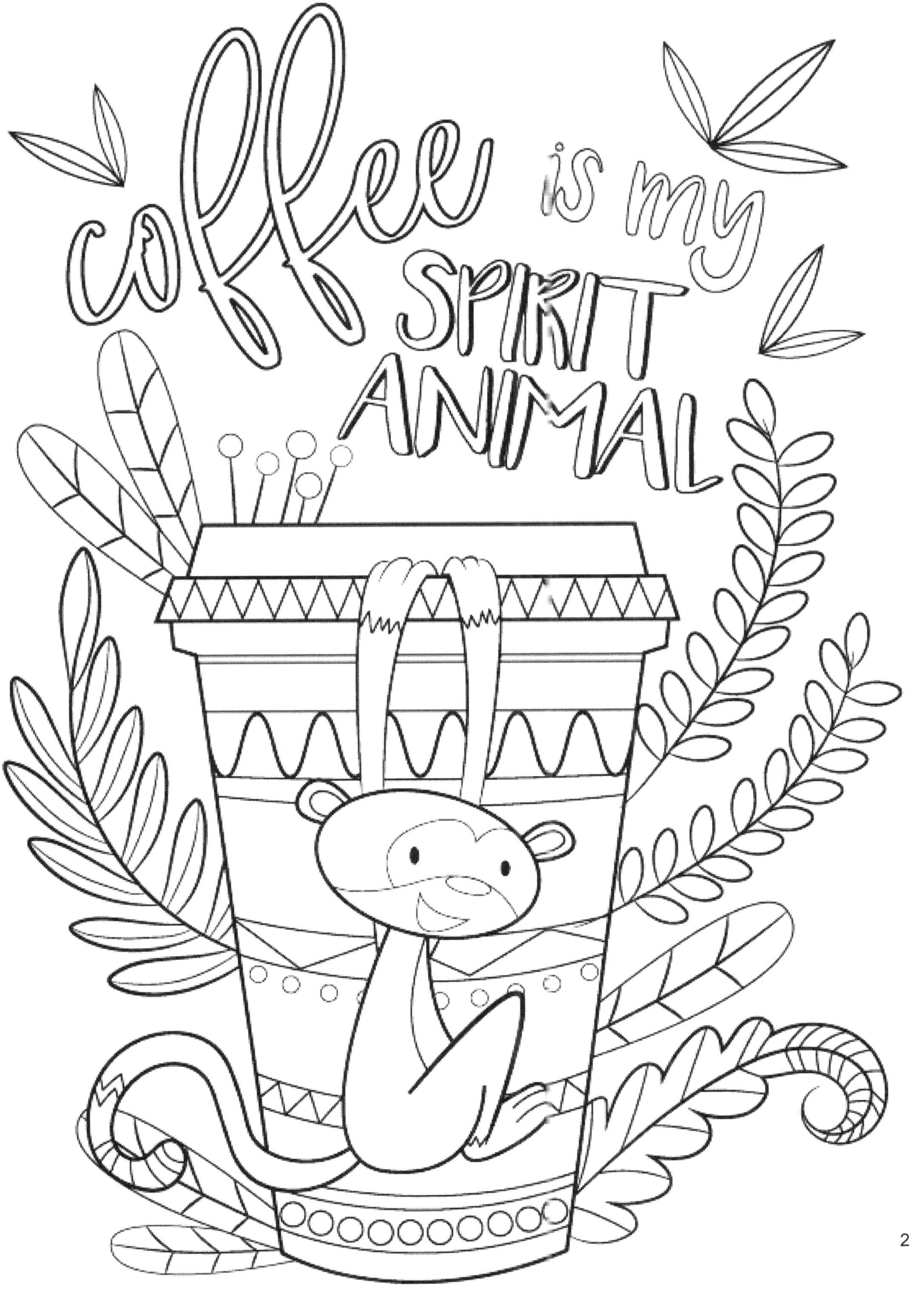
coffee is my
SPIRIT
ANIMAL

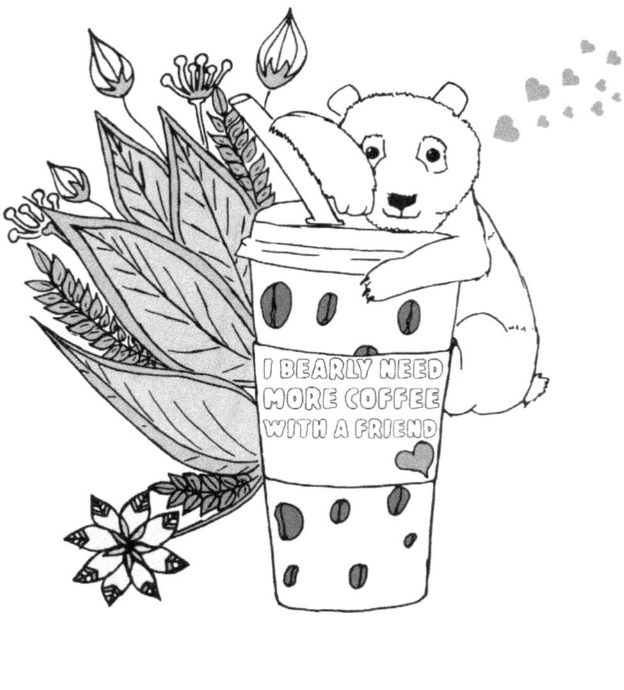
I BEARLY NEED
MORE COFFEE
WITH A FRIEND

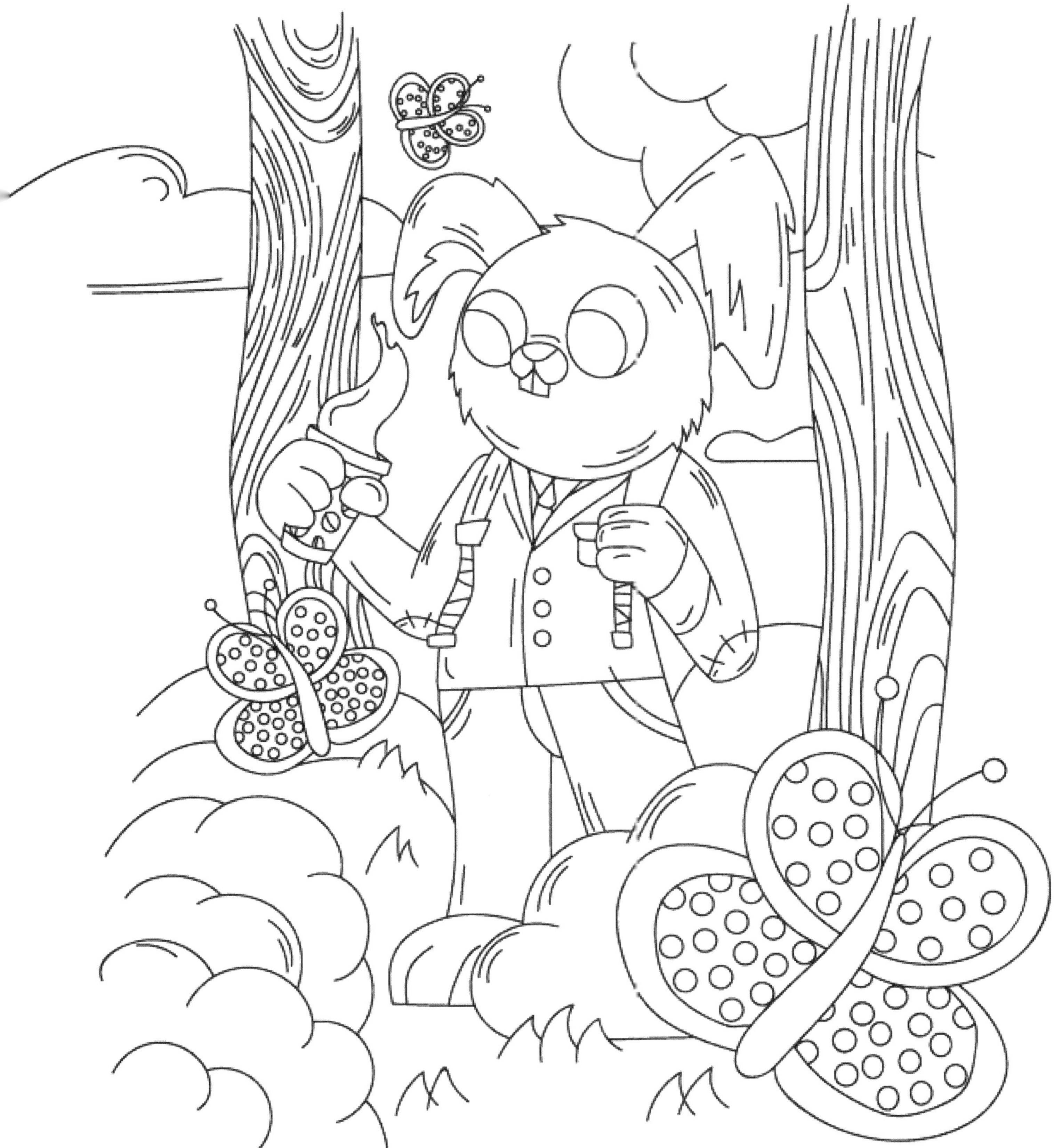

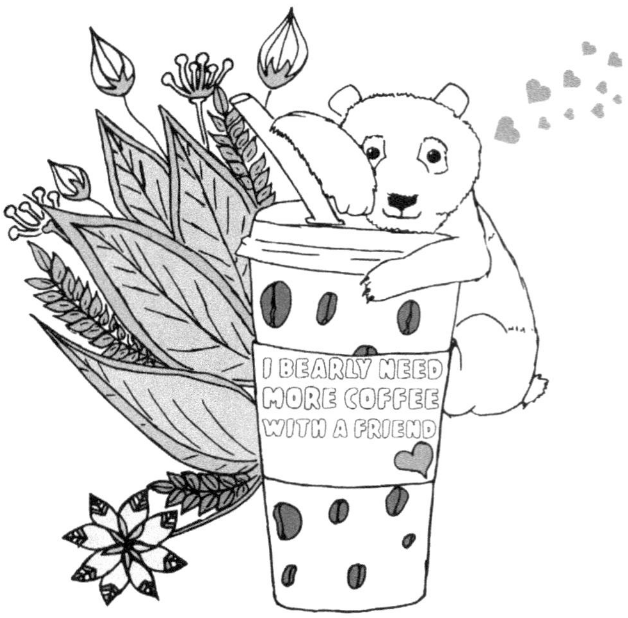
I BEARLY NEED
MORE COFFEE
WITH A FRIEND

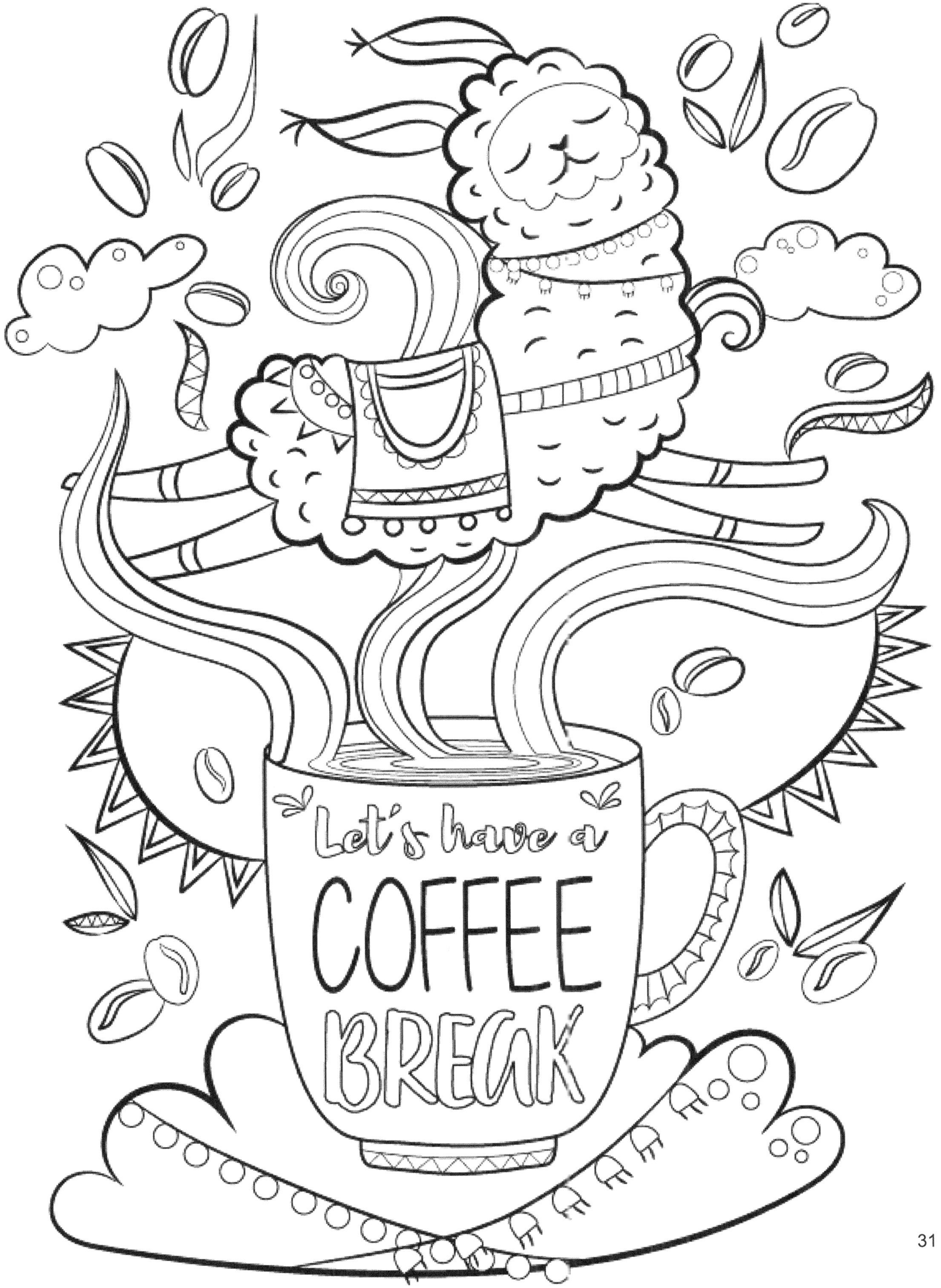
Let's have a
COFFEE
BREAK

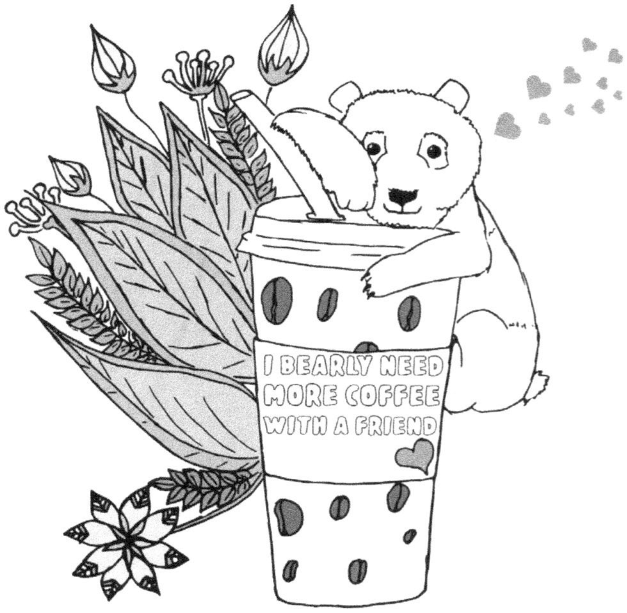
I BEARLY NEED
MORE COFFEE
WITH A FRIEND

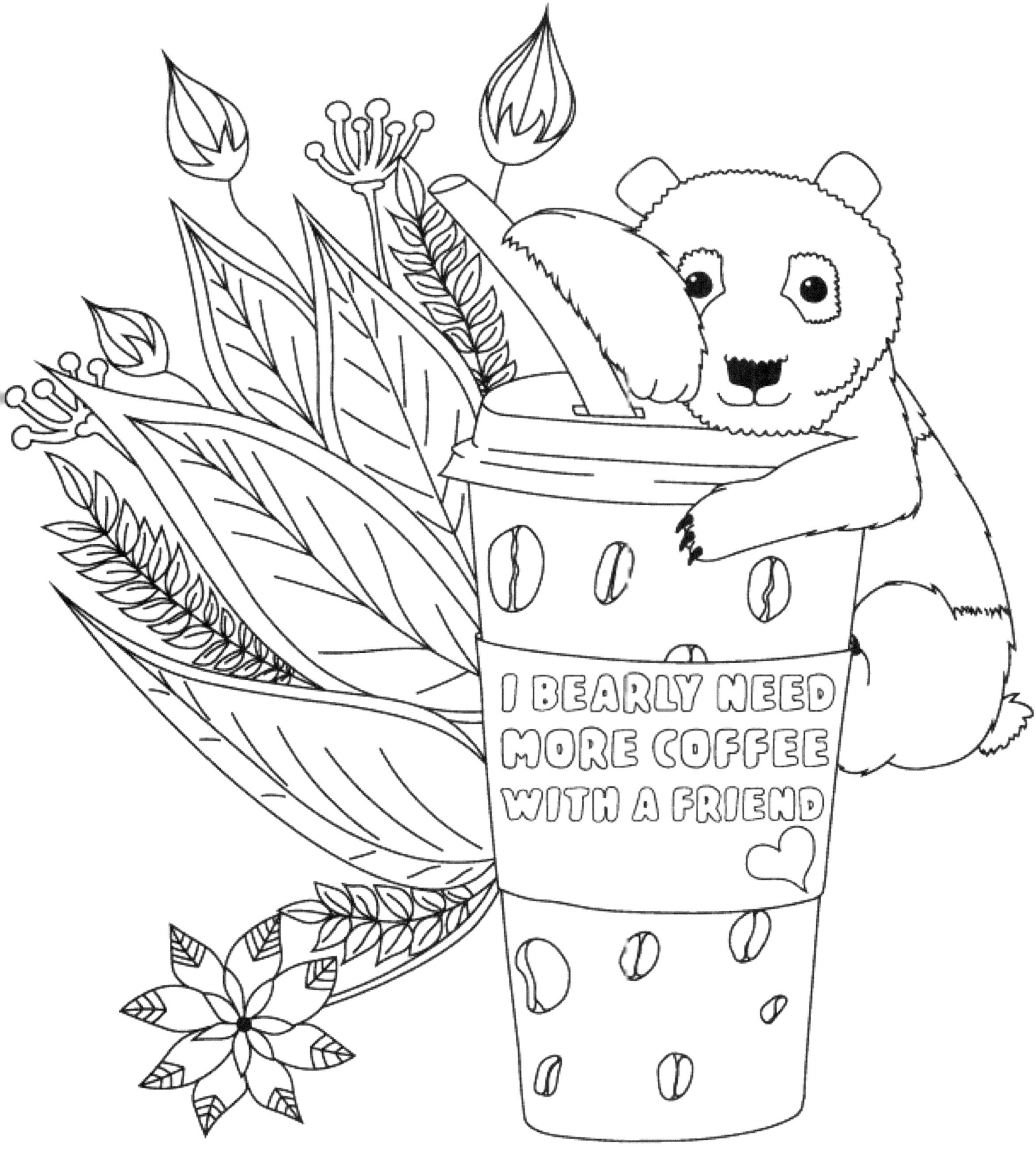
I BEARLY NEED
MORE COFFEE
WITH A FRIEND

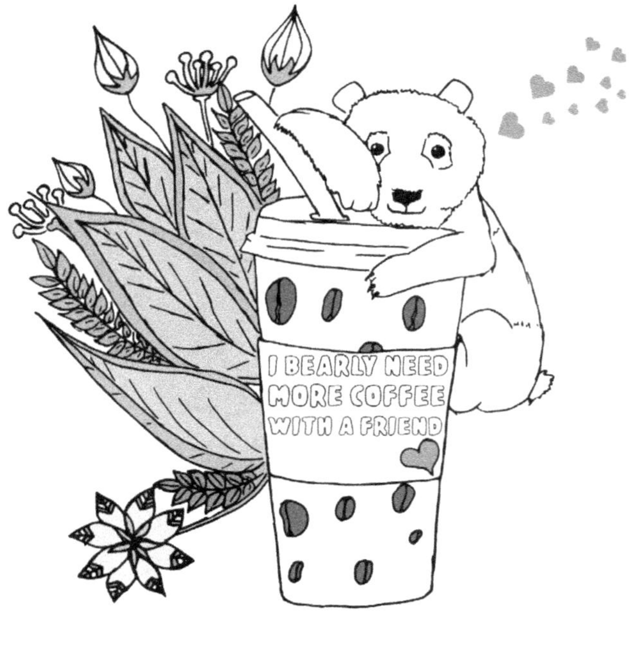
I BEARLY NEED
MORE COFFEE
WITH A FRIEND

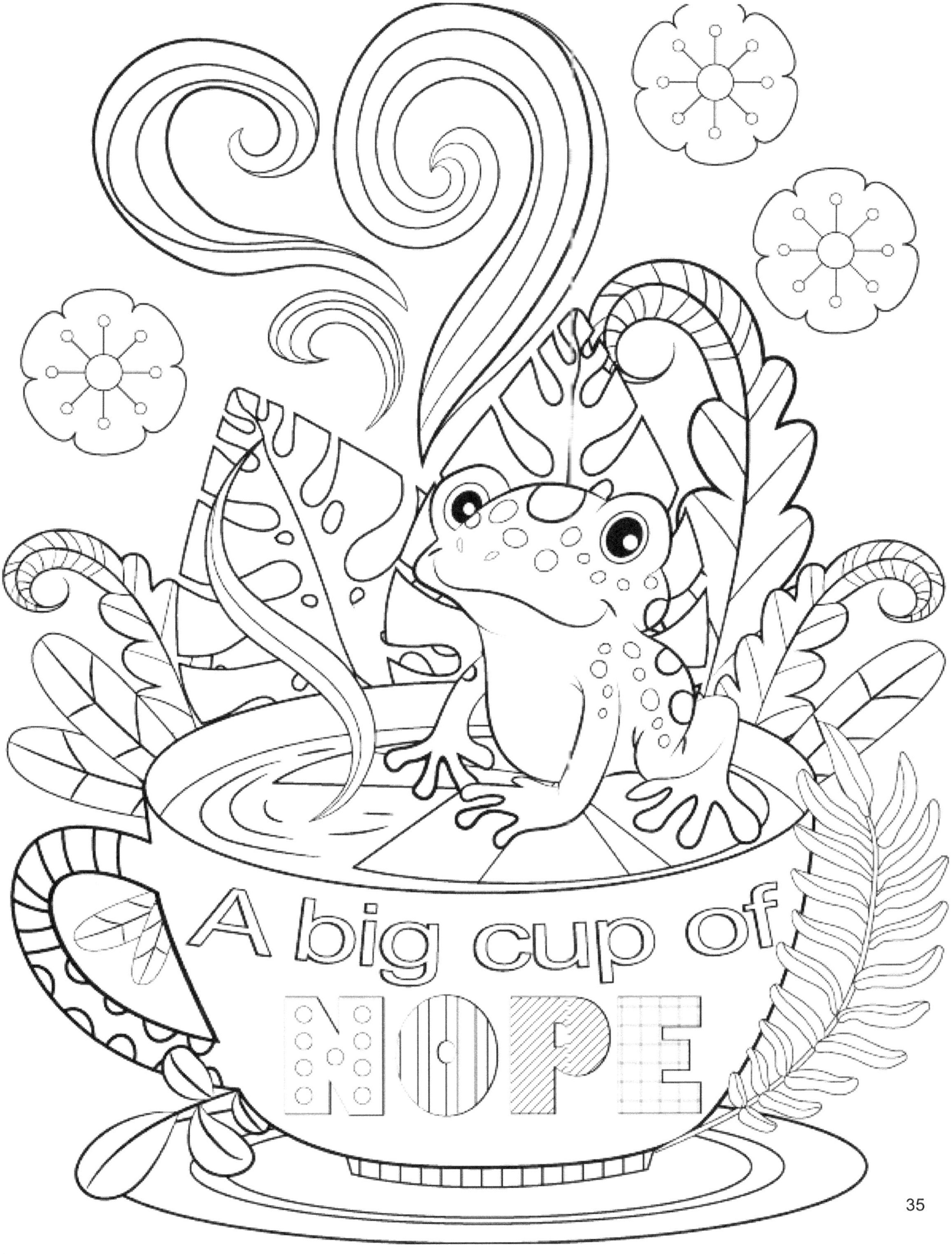
A big cup of
NOPE

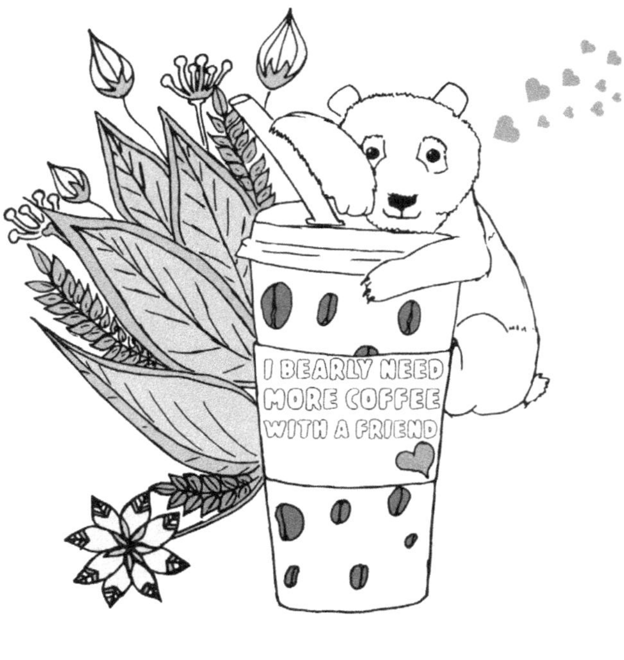
I BEARLY NEED
MORE COFFEE
WITH A FRIEND

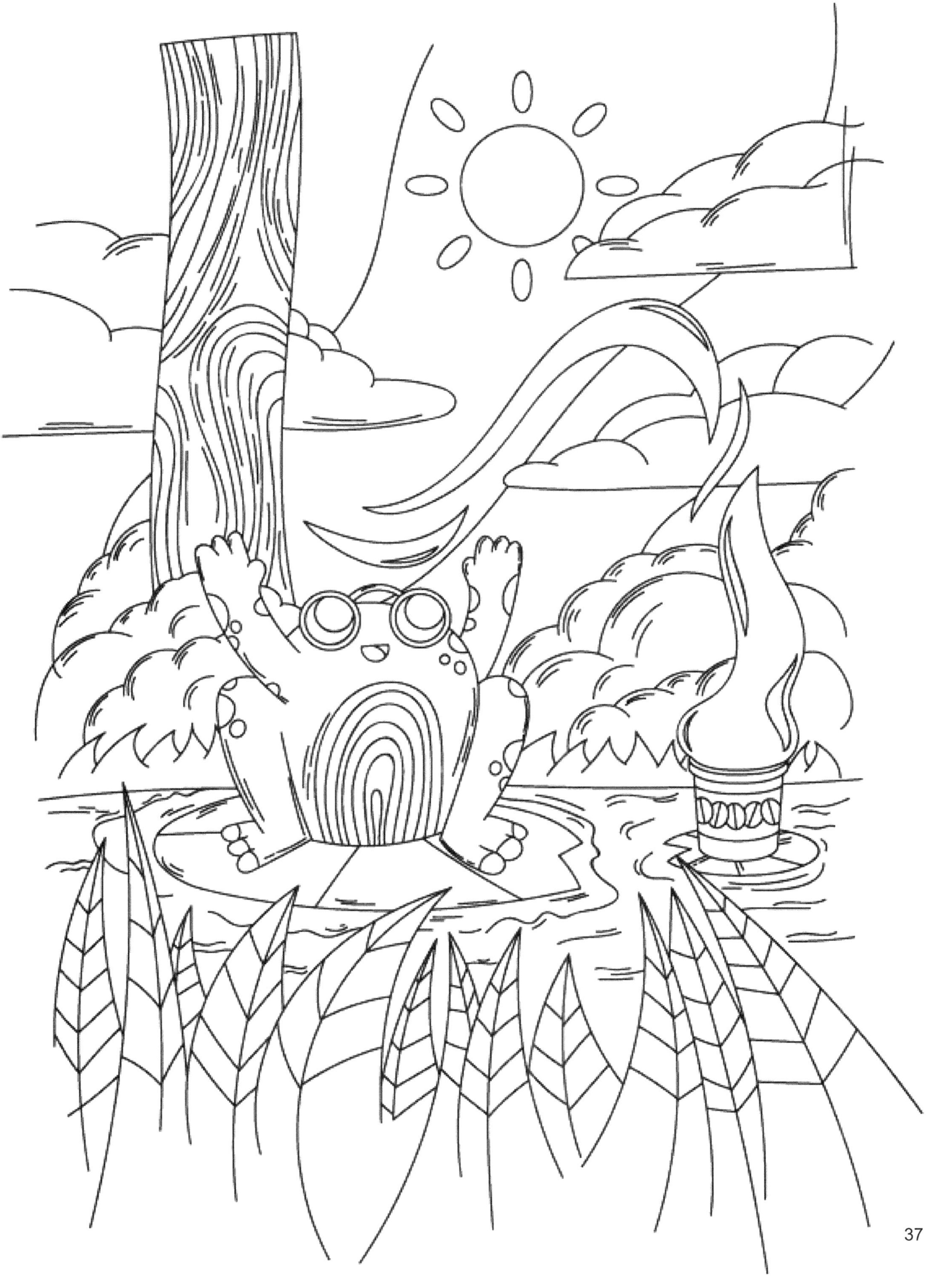

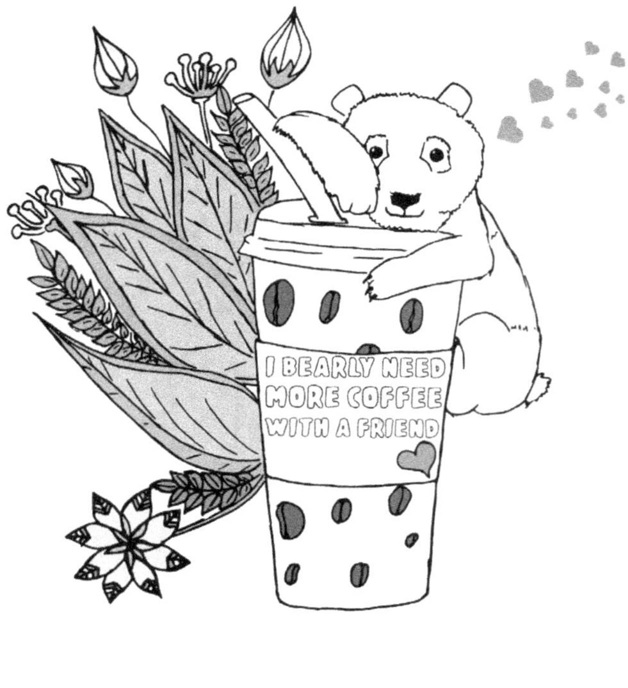
I BEARLY NEED
MORE COFFEE
WITH A FRIEND

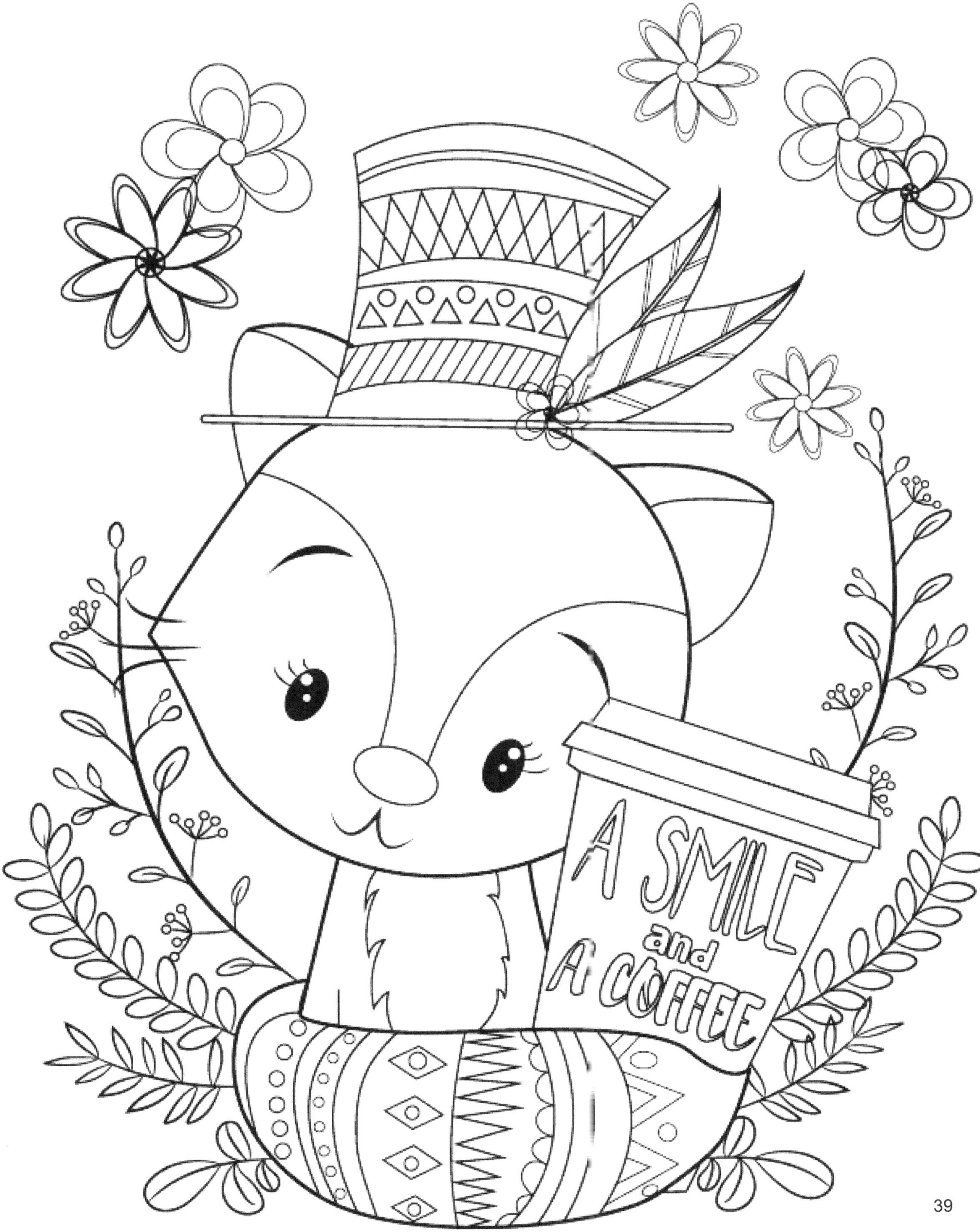
A SMILE
and
A COFFEE

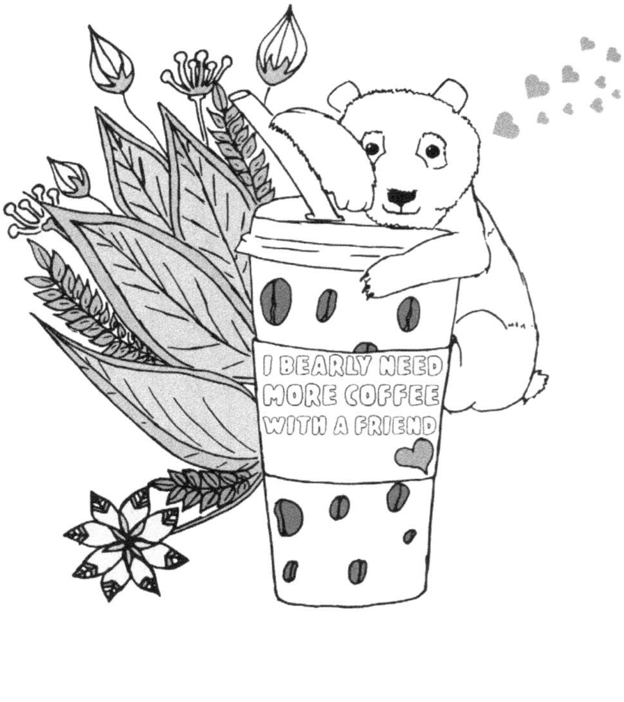
I BEARLY NEED
MORE COFFEE
WITH A FRIEND

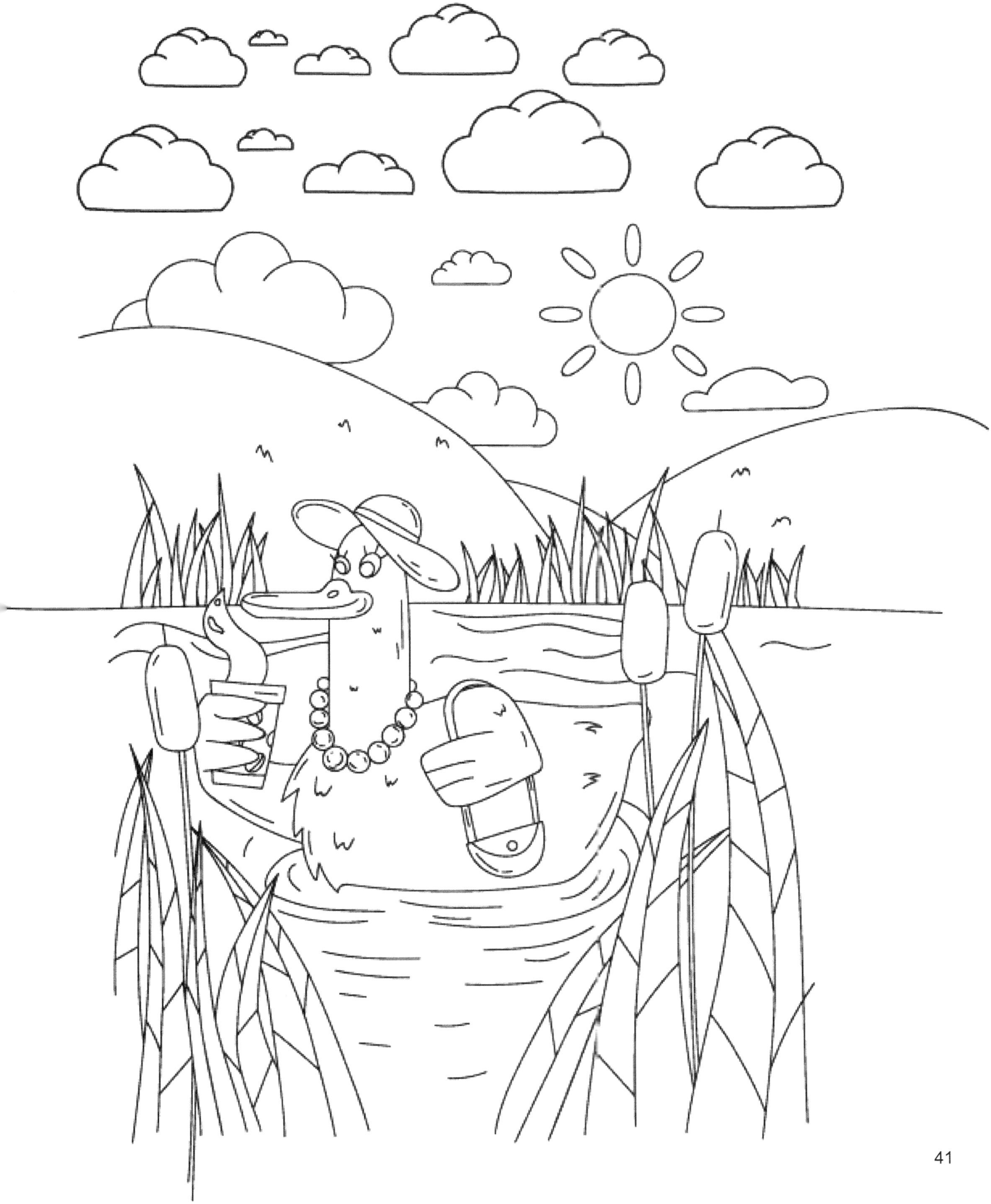

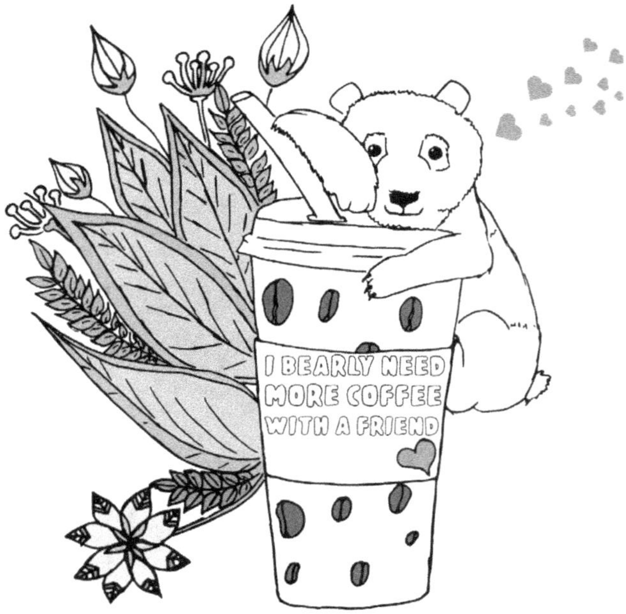
I BEARLY NEED
MORE COFFEE
WITH A FRIEND

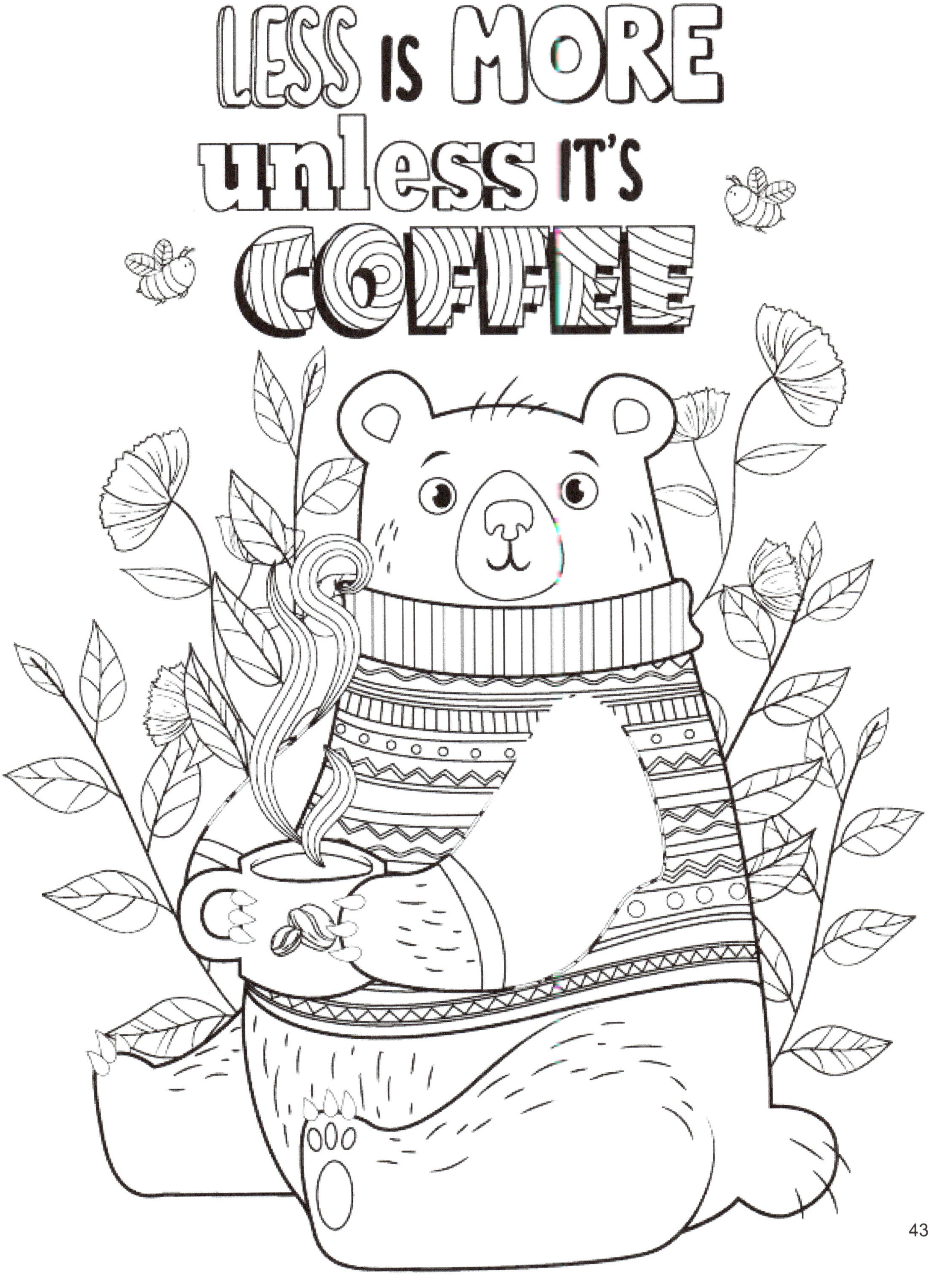
LESS IS MORE
unless IT'S
COFFEE

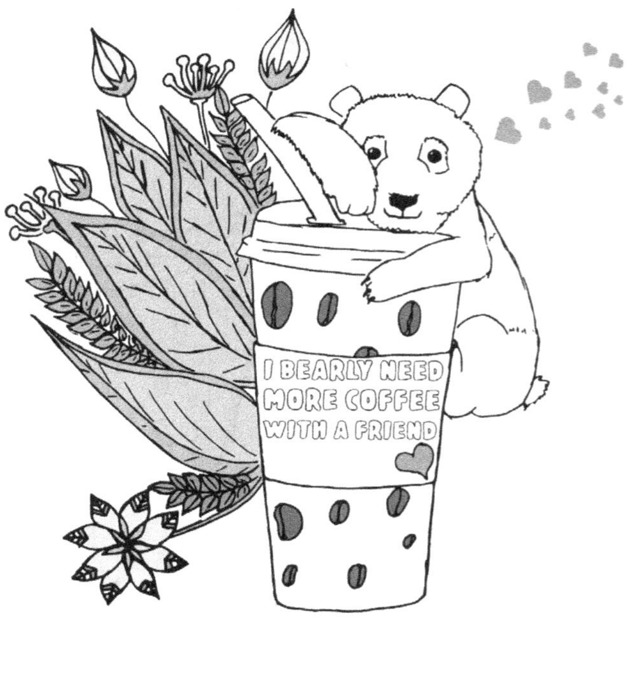
I BEARLY NEED
MORE COFFEE
WITH A FRIEND

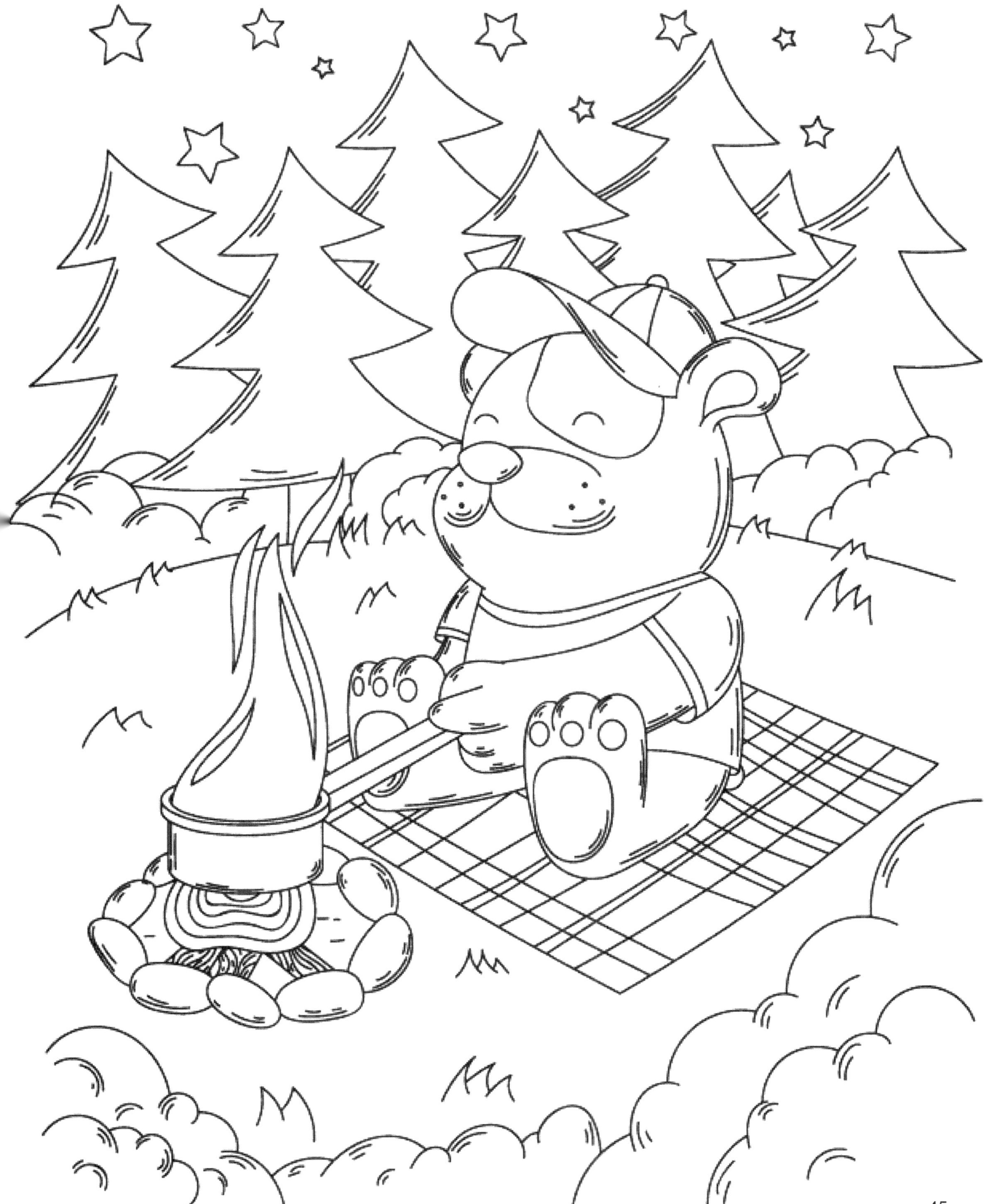

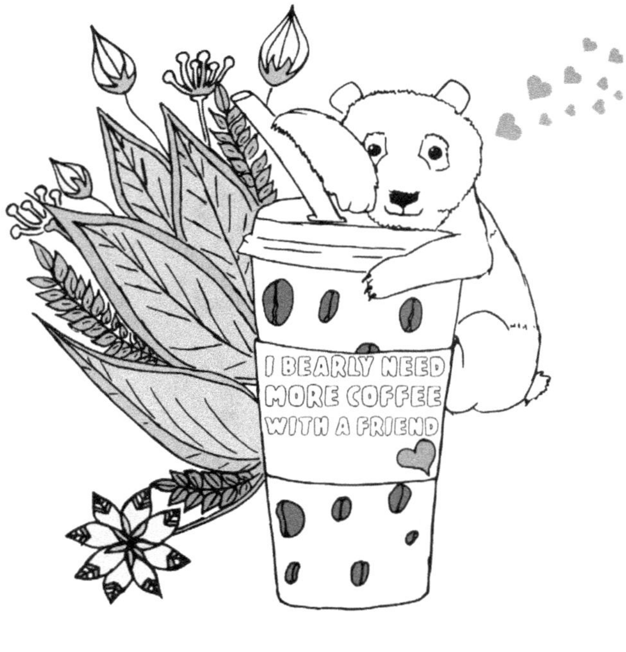
I BEARLY NEED
MORE COFFEE
WITH A FRIEND

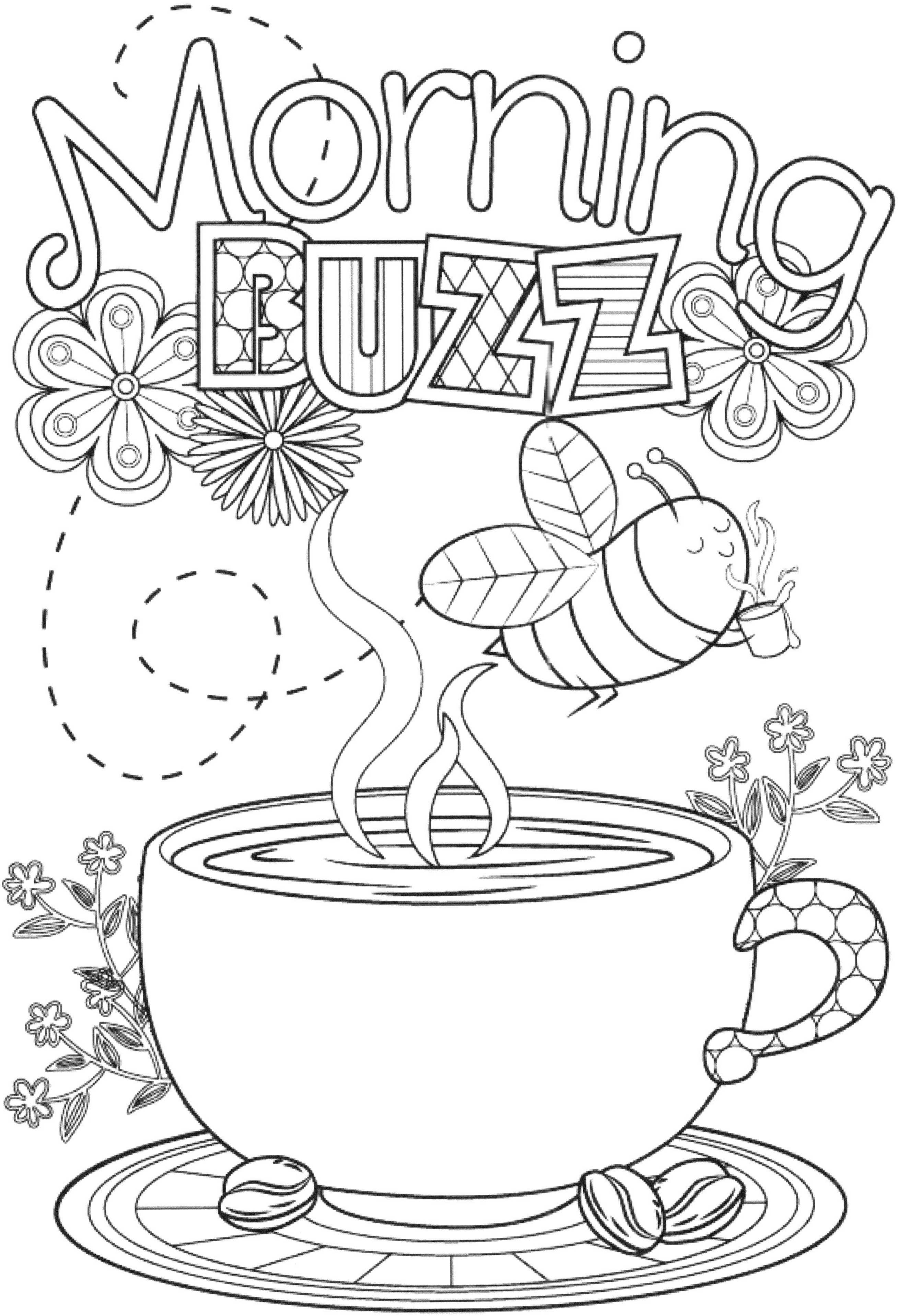
Morning
BUZZZ

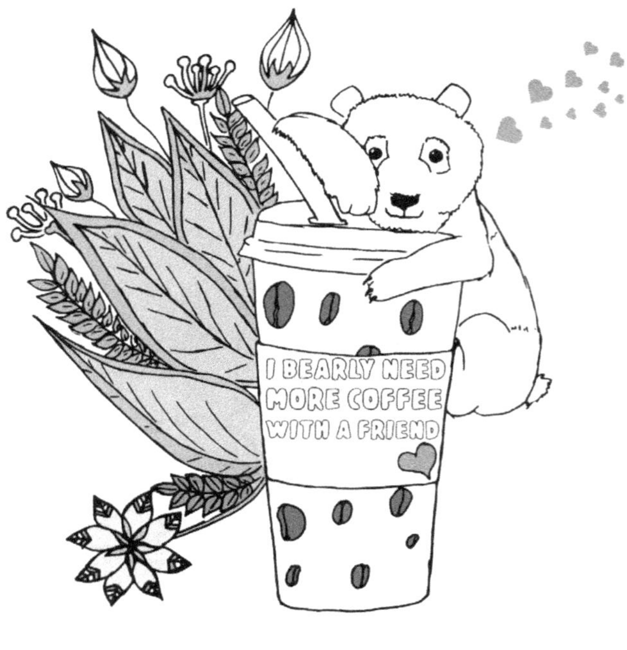
I BEARLY NEED
MORE COFFEE
WITH A FRIEND

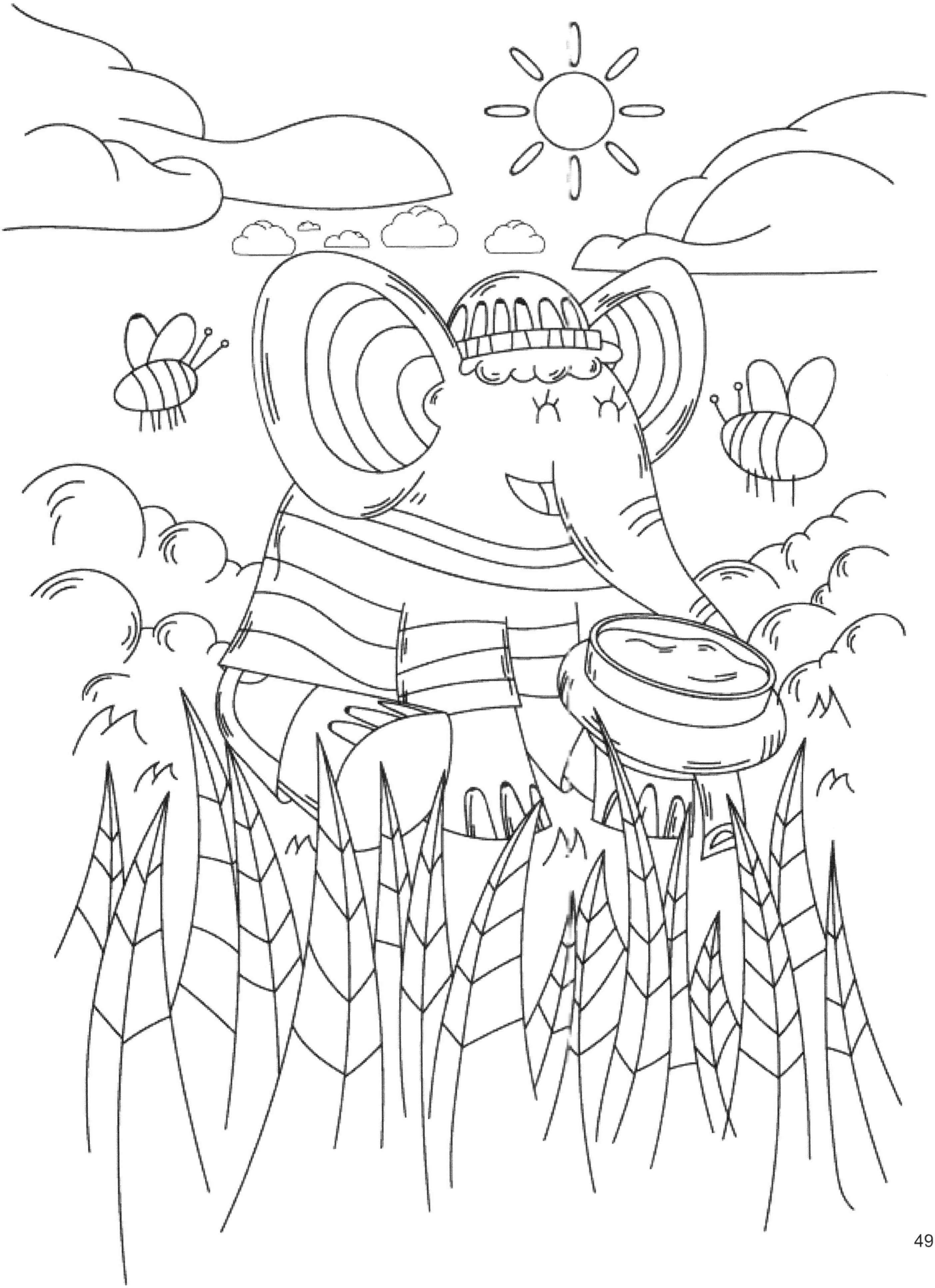

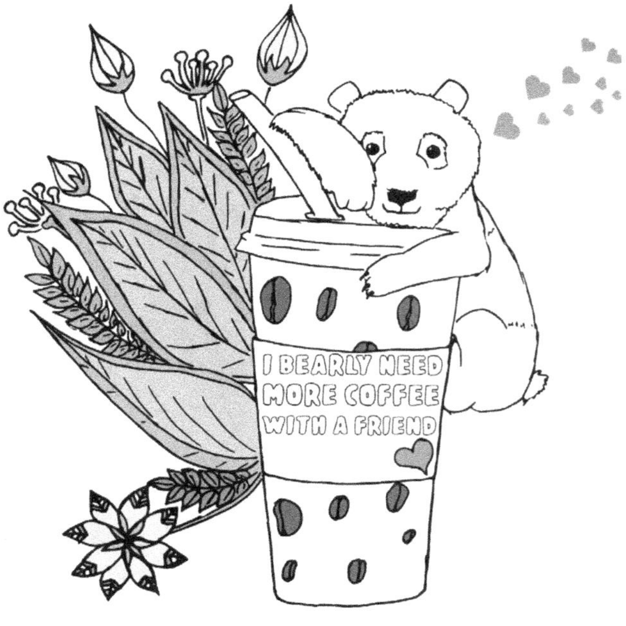
I BEARLY NEED
MORE COFFEE
WITH A FRIEND

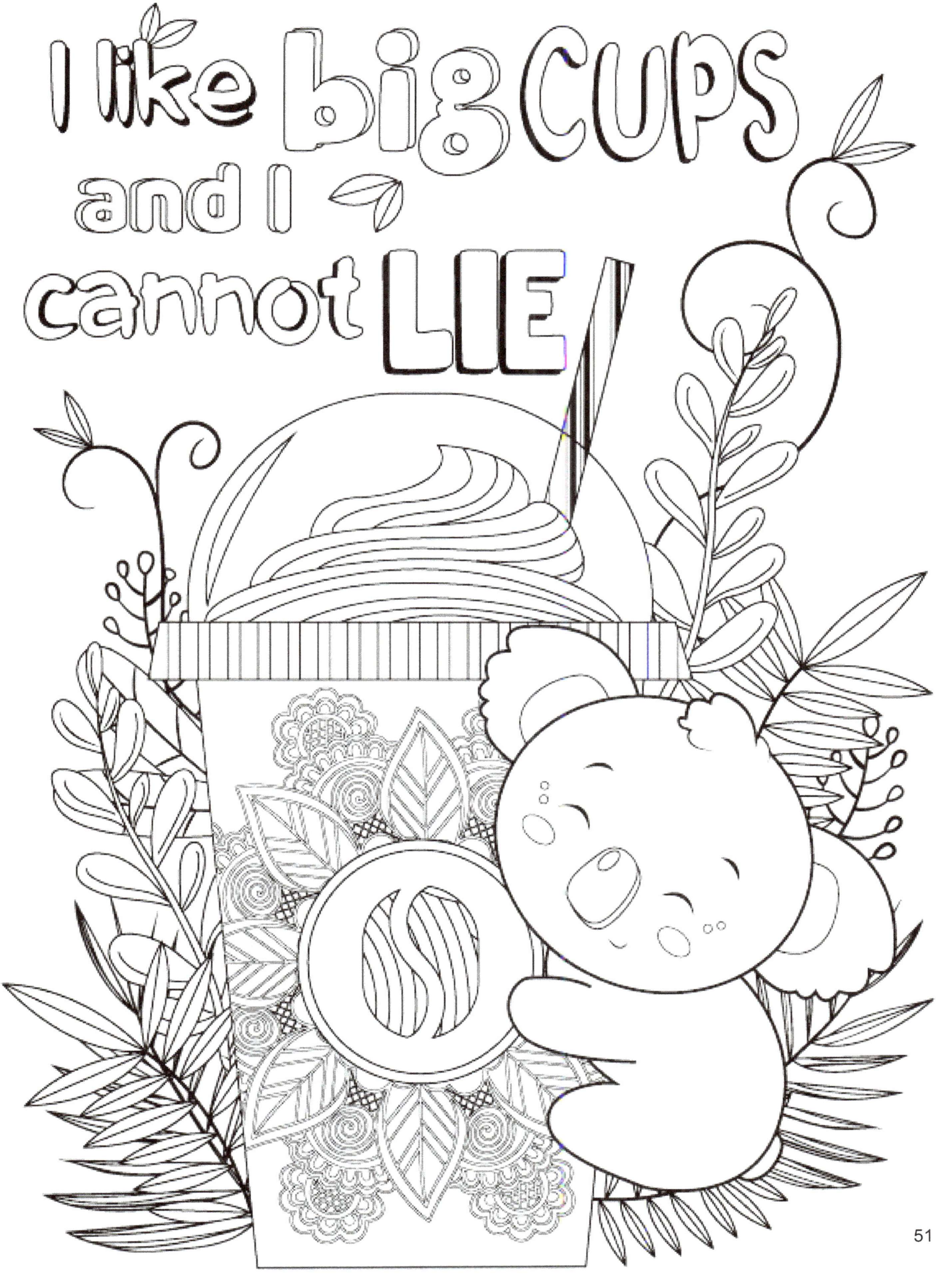
I like big CUPS
and I
cannot LIE

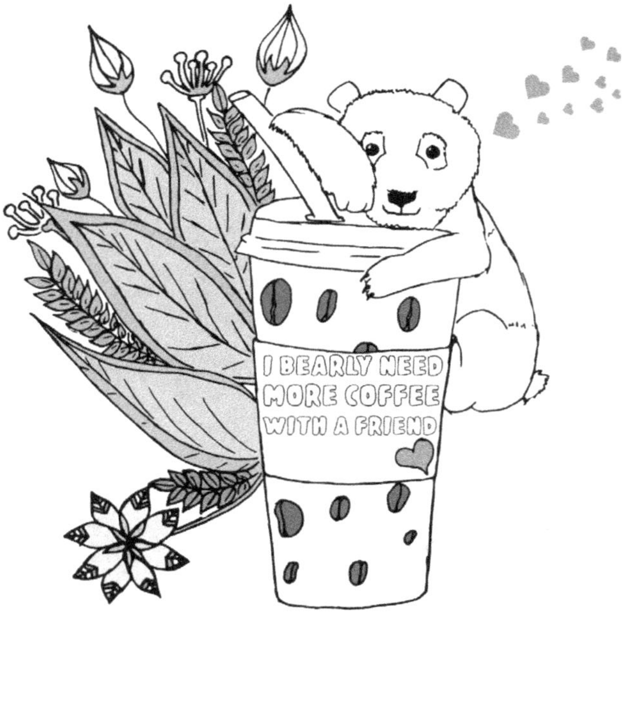
I BEARLY NEED
MORE COFFEE
WITH A FRIEND

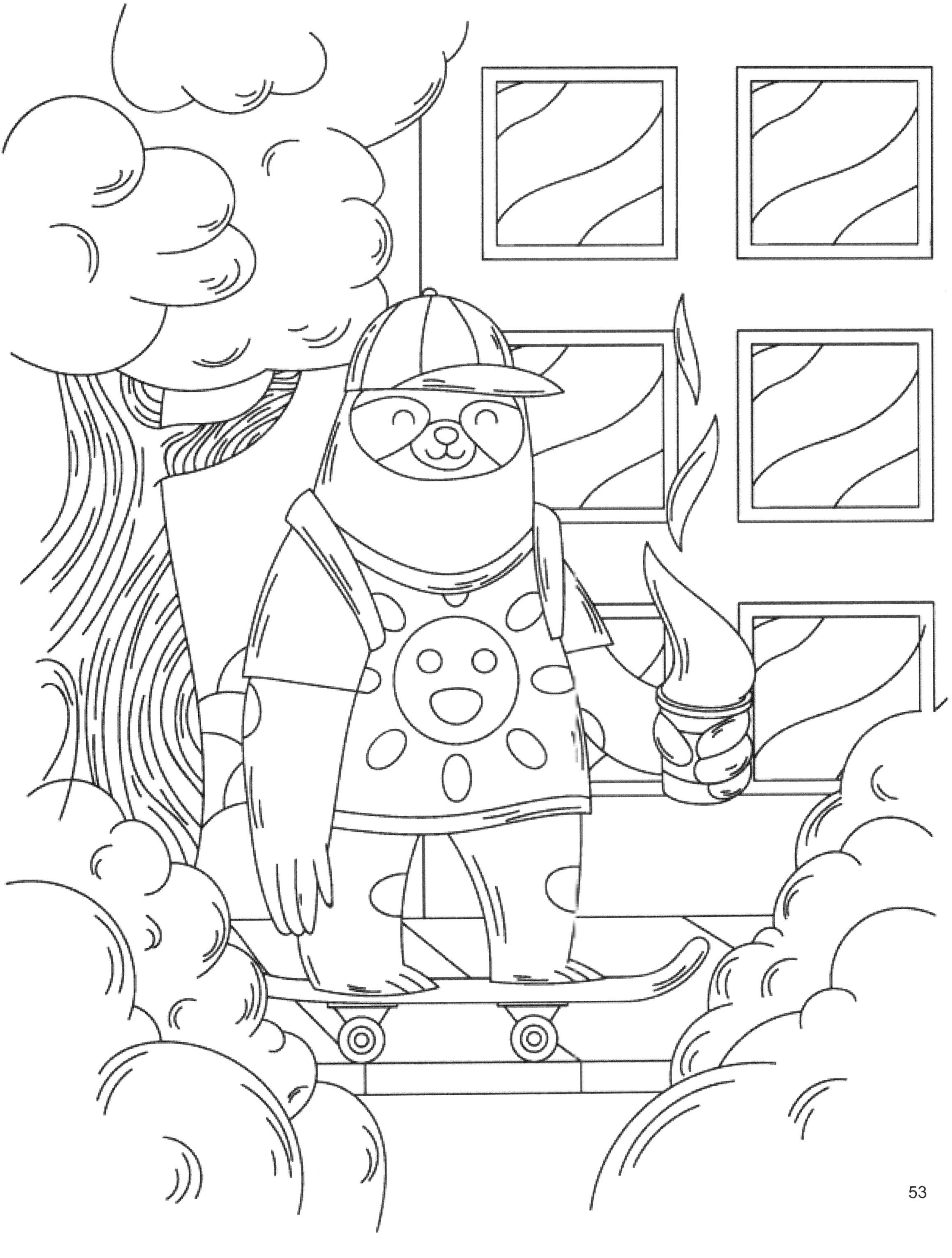

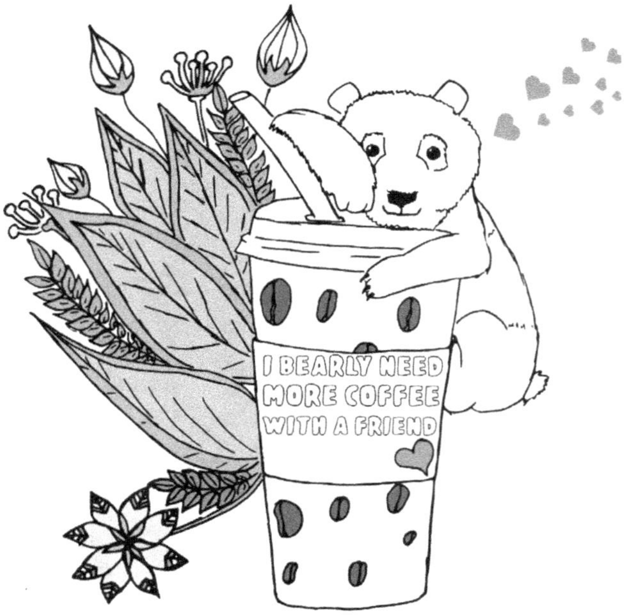
I BEARLY NEED
MORE COFFEE
WITH A FRIEND

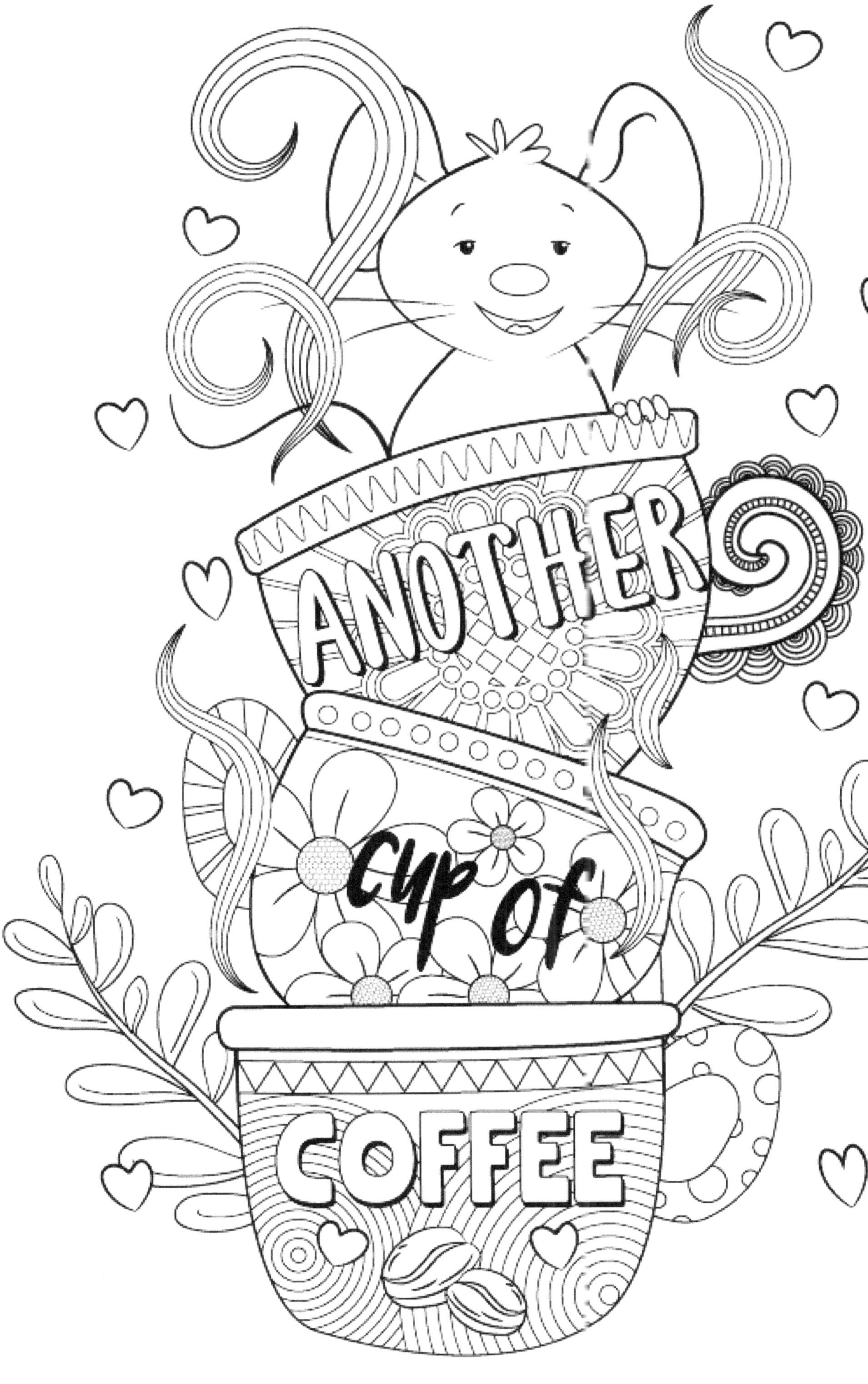
ANOTHER
cup of
COFFEE

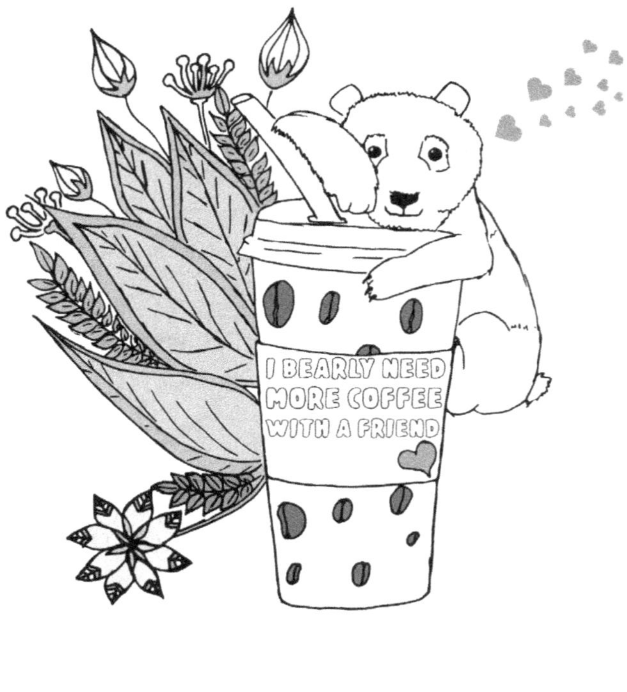
I BEARLY NEED
MORE COFFEE
WITH A FRIEND

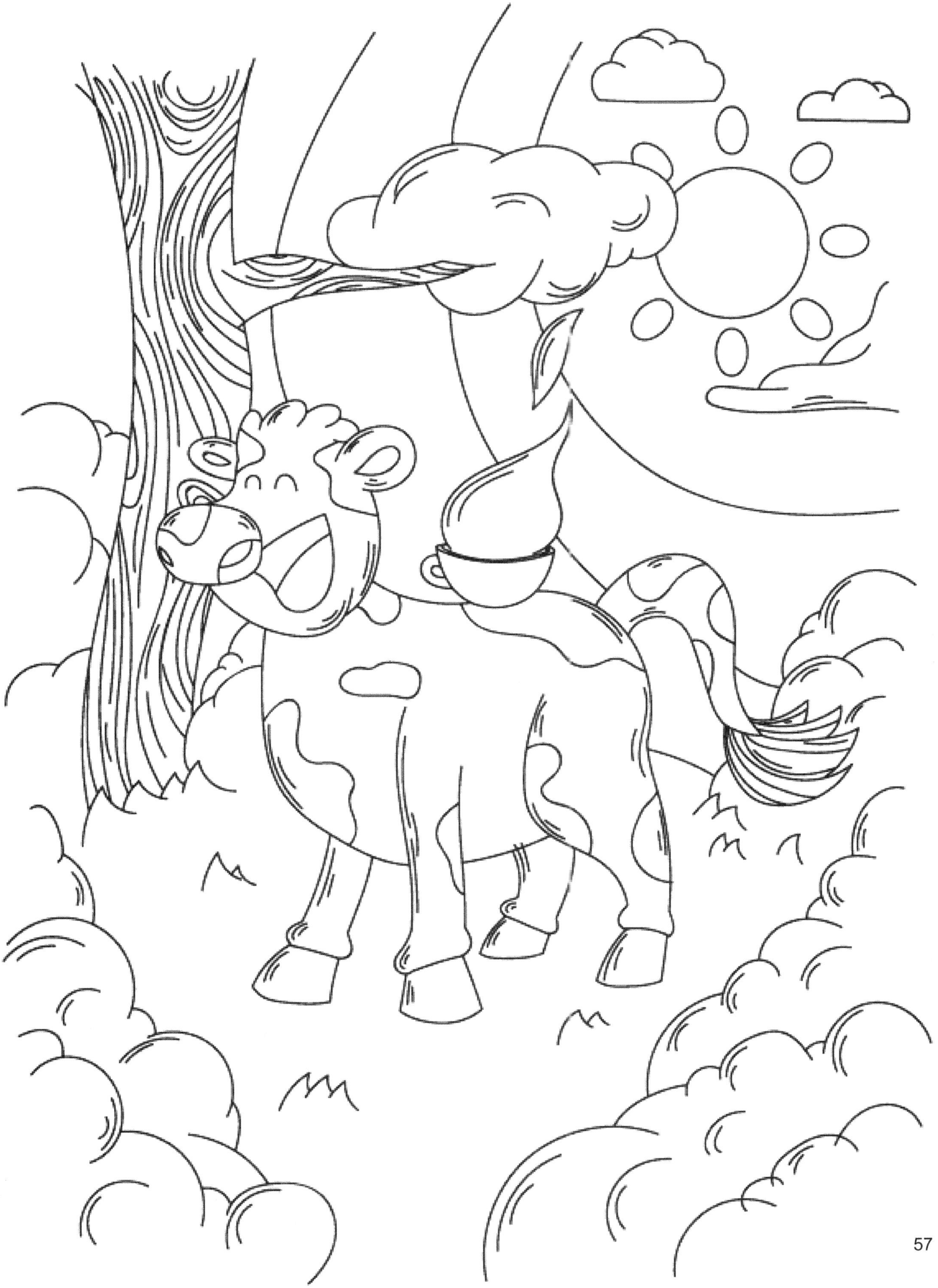

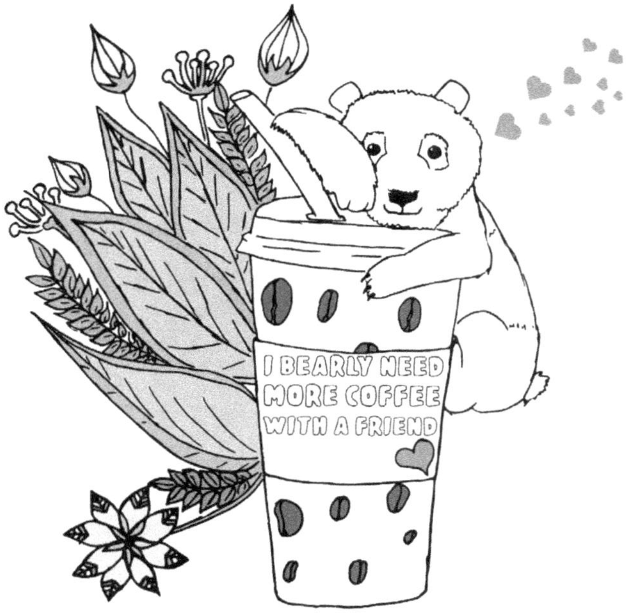
I BEARLY NEED
MORE COFFEE
WITH A FRIEND

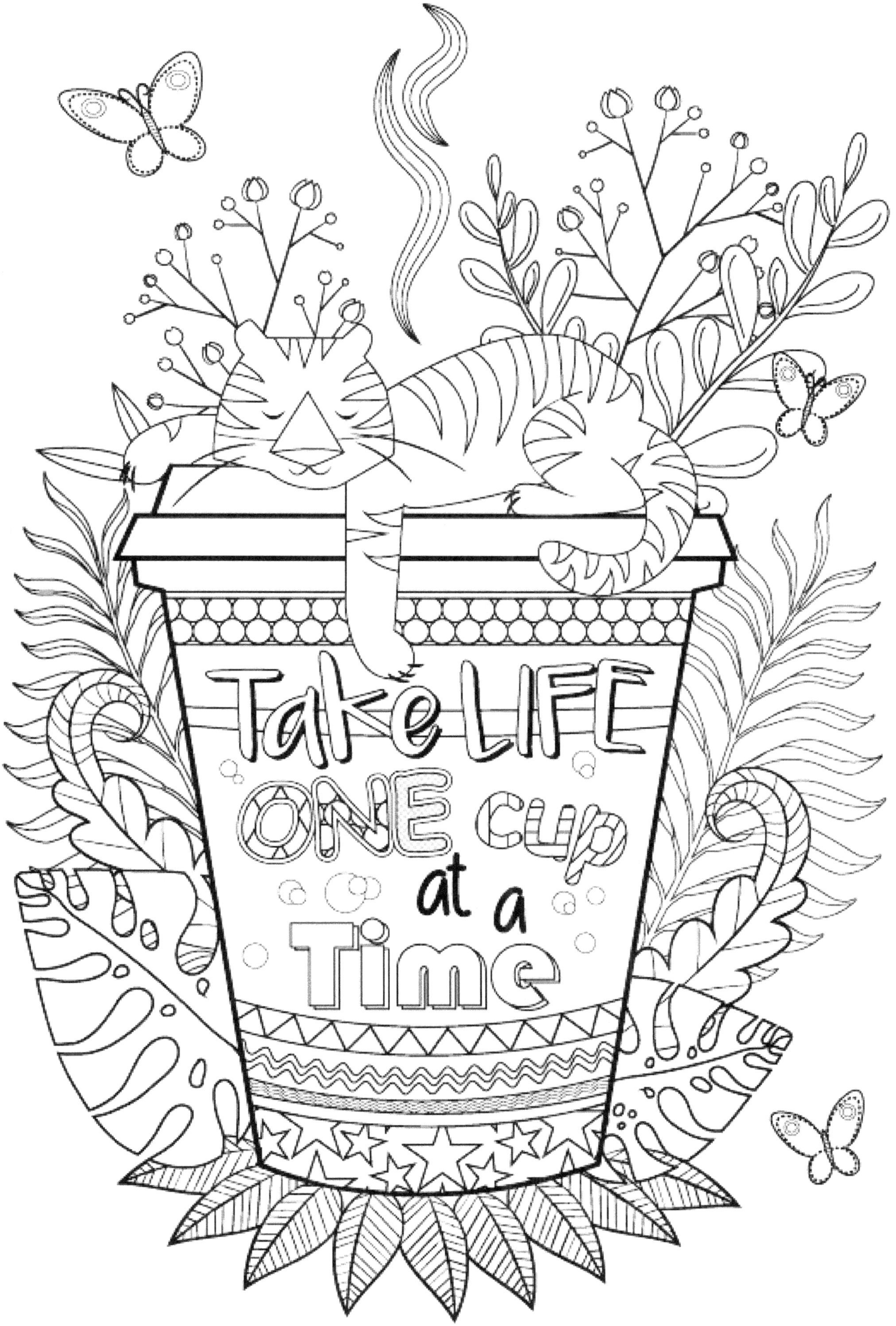
Take LIFE
ONE cup
at a
Time

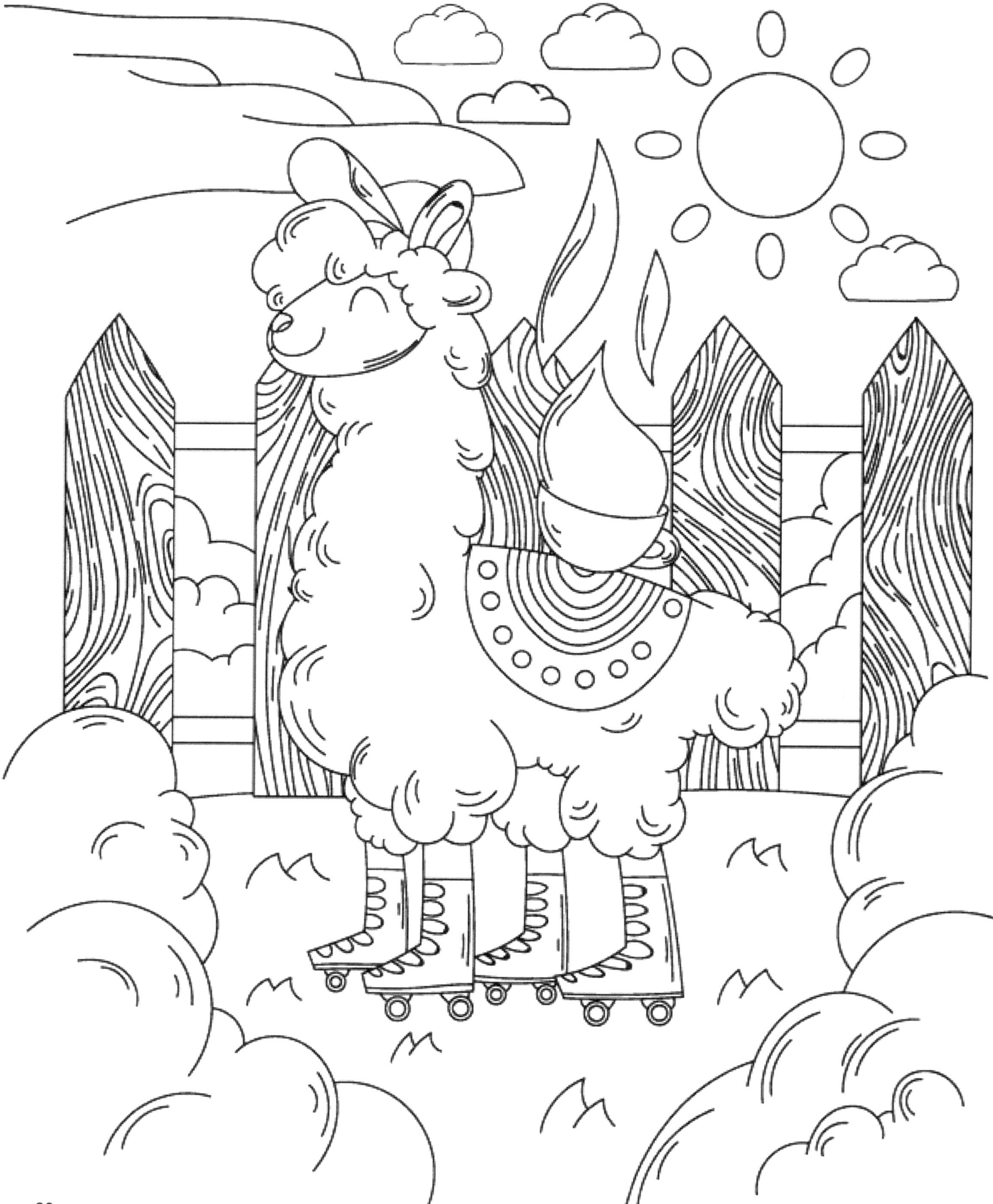

www.ingramcontent.com/pod-product-compliance
Lightning Source LLC
Chambersburg PA
CBHW060442220526
45465CB00008B/3238
9798645883102